HIGH
PERFORMANCE
The Daily Journal

HIGH
PERFORMANCE
The Daily Journal

365 Ways to Become Your Best

Jake Humphrey

Cornerstone Press

1 3 5 7 9 10 8 6 4 2

Cornerstone Press
20 Vauxhall Bridge Road
London SW1V 2SA

Cornerstone Press is part of the Penguin Random House group of companies
whose addresses can be found at global.penguinrandomhouse.com

Penguin
Random House
UK

This book incorporates material originally published in
High Performance: Lessons from the Best on Becoming Your Best,
published by Random House Business in 2021.

First published by Cornerstone Press in 2022

www.penguin.co.uk

A CIP catalogue record for this book is available from the British Library.

ISBN 9781529902563

Typeset in 11/14.5pt Sabon GEO by Jouve (UK), Milton Keynes
Printed and bound in Great Britain by Clays Ltd, Elcograf S.p.A.

The authorised representative in the EEA is Penguin Random House
Ireland, Morrison Chambers, 32 Nassau Street, Dublin D02 YH68.

www.greenpenguin.co.uk

CONTENTS

PREFACE: 365 DAYS

High Performers,

Welcome to the only journal you will ever need. This book is the next step on your journey to high performance. It is your new best friend. You will go everywhere together. You will share everything.

I've long known that writing things down can change your life. I was journalling before I even knew what 'journalling' was. Since secondary school I have been making notes, creating lists and leaving myself reminders and notes of encouragement. Every worthwhile achievement in my life was written down before it was realised. From my TV career to my children, from the business I founded to the podcast so many of you love – they all began with short, written notes.

Worry not: this is not a guide to 'manifesting'. I am not saying that by writing something down it *will* happen. However, I believe that when you write something down it becomes more *likely* to happen. Putting your ideas in writing is like creating a contract. Once your thoughts are on a piece of paper you feel compelled to act upon them. I am not alone. Everyone from the world's greatest sportspeople to billionaire business leaders have come on the *High Performance* podcast to tell us about the power of note-making to change your situation.

As such, this book is made up of 52 weeks' worth of practical exercises, each offering seven meditations on motivation, success or teamwork. Every week begins with a few simple, repeated questions that are designed to get you thinking about your priorities for the seven days ahead. The end result is 365 nuggets of inspiration – one for every day of the year.

These nuggets fall into one of three categories. First, *Inspire*: short, inspirational quotes from the planet's greatest sportspeople, coaches and psychologists. Second, *Think*. This is where your pen comes in handy – these are simple prompts that invite you to reflect on your day, your work and your life. And finally, *Do*: hands-on exercises that invite you to scribble in your ideas, which will help you identify your strengths and hone your skills.

The book is divided into eight lessons, which mirrors the structure of the original *High Performance* book (and I'd encourage you to read the two books side by side). But between each lesson, I've included some completely new material: 'In Focus' weeks that home in on specific elements of your journey – whether diet, exercise or rest – that I've never explored in writing before.

How you use this book is up to you. If you like, you can dive in at random and complete as many exercises a day as you see fit. Alternatively, you can use this journal as your map to a high-performance year. If you work through it every day, from front to back, then in 365 days you might just have changed your life.

I believe this is a journal unlike any other. It is as unique as you are, and will give you a deeper, more honest relationship with the most important person in your life: you.

Happy journalling,

Jake X

What is High Performance?

HIGH PERFORMANCE
FOR YOU

Welcome to *High Performance: The Daily Journal*. By picking up this book, you've taken the first step towards transforming your mindset, your behaviour and your life. Which elements of your life would you like to change?

_____

_____

_____

Later in the introduction, we'll help you to set your **goals** for the year. What would you like to get out of this book?

_____

_____

_____

This week's focus is **high performance for you**. We're going to explore what high performance means – and show that it can vary wildly from person to person. What does high performance mean to you?

_____

_____

_____

Think

When Damian and I started researching the *High Performance* podcast, we knew our guests would be far too diverse for there to be a single, all-encompassing definition of high performance. Having interviewed everyone from Premier League footballers to billionaire entrepreneurs, from ballet dancers to rugby league coaches, I can now say that we were right: there are many definitions of high performance. How do you define high performance?

_____

_____

_____

_____

_____

_____

_____

_____

_____

_____

_____

_____

_____

Inspire

'Success is only 20 per cent talent.'

Kelly Holmes, Olympic and Commonwealth
running champion

Do

While there may not be a single definition of high performance, high-achieving people tend to have a few recurrent characteristics. Think of three high-performing individuals you admire, and write the name of each one next to a circle below. Next, write the words you associate with each of them – 'hard-working', 'thoughtful', 'articulate' and so on – inside the relevant circles. If a word applies to more than one of them, write it in the overlapping areas. Are any characteristics shared by all your high performers?

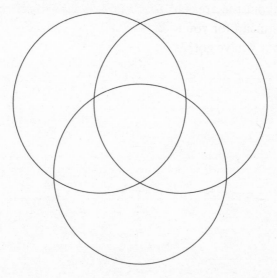

Inspire

'Do the best you can, where you are, with what you have got.'

Phil Neville, head coach of Inter Miami and former Manchester United, Everton and England footballer

Think

This quote from Phil Neville is the closest we've come to a catch-all definition of high performance. We like it because it can encompass people from all walks of life. If you work in business, it might involve investing extra time in polishing that important sales pitch. If the most important thing in your life is family, high performance might be as simple as spending quality time with the ones you love.

Think about the areas of your life you want to change. What would it mean for you to do the best you can, where you are, with what you've got?

_____

_____

_____

_____

_____

_____

_____

Do

Return to the three circles on page 4. Pick the three characteristics that you think would most help you on your high-performance journey, then label each bar below with one of the characteristics. Next, colour in the bars – the fuller the bar, the more you have the characteristic. What are the areas you need to do the most work in to become a high performer?

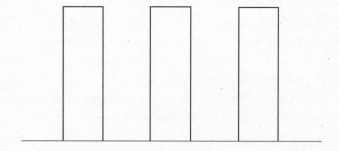

YOUR ANNUAL GOALS

Last week's focus was **high performance for you**. We explored how high performance differs from person to person – and tried to work out what it might mean in your life. What did you learn?

_____

_____

_____

Our focus this week is **your annual goals**. We're going to explore what good goals consist of and identify some for you. What does setting goals mean to you?

_____

_____

_____

Let's get started by **brainstorming your ideas** for your annual goals. Don't worry if you're not sure about them – just put down whatever comes to mind.

_____

_____

_____

Think

For many people, childhood dreams are a good starting point when working out ambitious goals for the future. At some point, we tend to abandon our childhood dreams – we get 'realistic'. But these dreams, however utopian, often tell us something about what we most value. Think back to your childhood and teenage years. What were your loftiest hopes and ambitions? Do these dreams still resonate today?

_____

_____

_____

_____

_____

_____

_____

_____

_____

_____

_____

_____

_____

_____

_____

Inspire

'Sometimes it feels like ambitions and goals are a big mountain. And in many respects, they are. But a mountain is moved one small pebble at a time.'

Steven Bartlett, award-winning entrepreneur and bestselling author

Do

The beauty entrepreneur Susie Ma once told us about the power of 'infinite purpose', which she developed based on a talk by the writer Simon Sinek. She focuses on goals that can scale up forever, without limit – which, in her case, involve creating a healthier, greener and more empowered world.

In the cloud below, write down the most ambitious, infinite goals you dare think of. Be as utopian as you like: improving the life of everyone on the planet, saving the environment, transforming every element of society. Once you've finished, reflect on what a smaller, more immediate version of these goals might look like. If saving the world was the end result, what would be a useful first step?

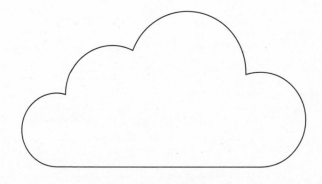

Inspire

'It's important to dream – to aspire to greatness.'

Sam Heughan, actor, entrepreneur and philanthropist

Do

In one of our favourite studies, researchers set out to explore what made various companies perform at a high level. Although all the organisations had clear goals, what set the highest-performing ones apart was their approach to setting goals. Instead of goals related to outcomes – like hitting a sales target or winning over a client – they set goals related to behaviours, like turning up on time or dressing smartly. The lesson of the study is simple: the best goals are focused not on outcomes, but on behaviours.

In the table, write down the outcomes you'd like to achieve in the next year. Then write down the behavioural goals that you think will help you achieve them.

	The year ahead
Outcome	
Behaviour	

Think

Write down your goals for the next year. Remember what we've learnt in this chapter. First, your goals should be ambitious – try to approach setting them with a sense of childlike wonder. Second, the best goals are focused not on outcomes but on behaviours. Finally, try to make your goals concrete: it should be self-evident what each one means, even to a stranger.

Take your time writing your goals. It's important to get them right, as we'll be referring back to your goals throughout the year.

Responsibility

THE POWER OF RESPONSIBILITY

Last week's focus was **your annual goals**. We explored how the best goals are ambitious, concrete and focused on behaviours rather than on outcomes. What did you learn?

Think about your **goals** for the year. What will you do this week to help you achieve them?

This week's focus is **the power of responsibility**. It will show you the importance of taking responsibility for every aspect of your life – even the parts that seem like they're outside your control. What does responsibility mean to you?

Inspire

'I feel like you have to be able to take responsibility as a person first, before pointing the finger at anybody else.'

Osi Umenyiora, former NFL player and two-time Super Bowl winner

Think

The legendary psychologist Albert Bandura was obsessed with the idea of 'self-efficacy'. He argued that when people don't believe they have what it takes to complete a task successfully, they see little point in making an initial effort. He referred to this as 'low self-efficacy'. The opposite, when people start out believing they can achieve things, is 'high self-efficacy'. People with high self-efficacy, Bandura believed, tend to have better life outcomes – and high self-efficacy is something that can be learned. Think about your own experiences: do you have low or high self-efficacy?

_____

_____

_____

_____

_____

_____

Do

The trick to building high self-efficacy, Bandura believed, is taking responsibility for your life. This exercise will help you do so. In the first column, write down some of your short-term goals. In the second column, write down what you feel is preventing you from achieving them. Now, reframe it: next to the words, 'I can . . .' write down something about the situation that *is* in your control. The lesson is simple: people with high self-efficacy tend to put success or failure down to their own actions. They take 100 per cent responsibility for themselves.

Goal	Obstacle
I want . . .	*I can . . .*

Inspire

'I knew it wasn't my fault. But how I reacted was my responsibility.'

Billy Monger, F4 driver who continued to race after a life-changing crash

Do

When high performers encounter setbacks that are beyond their control, they remember that there's one thing they *can* control: their response. As Billy Monger taught us, this is a matter of 'fault vs responsibility': just because something isn't our *fault* doesn't mean that it's not our *responsibility* to respond as well as we can.

Think about your reaction to a setback in your life. Would you react the same way again? What could you have done differently if you had been focused on taking responsibility?

The setback	Reaction
	I did . . . *I should have . . .*

Think

When things go wrong, it's human to look for someone to blame. But blame is useless. All that matters is how we respond. We call this the No Blame Principle. Reflect on a time when you blamed someone else for a bad situation. Now, recount the story as though you'd applied the No Blame Principle. What would have gone differently?

_____

_____

_____

_____

_____

_____

_____

_____

_____

_____

_____

_____

_____

_____

_____

_____

_____

WHAT CAN YOU CONTROL?

Last week's focus was **the power of responsibility.** We explored the differences between high and low self-efficacy and showed that high performers always take responsibility for what happens to them. What did you learn?

_____

_____

_____

Think about your **goals** for the year. What have you done in the past week to help you achieve them?

_____

_____

_____

This week's focus is **what can you control?** A key element of taking responsibility is focusing less on the things in your life that you can't control – and more on the things that you can. What does being in control mean to you?

_____

_____

_____

Inspire

'With experience you learn to worry about the things you can control and not the things that you can't.'

Christian Horner, team principal of Red Bull F1 and winner of nine world titles

Think

Think about your goals and what prevents you from achieving them. Now, identify the tangible steps you can take towards achieving them. The only person who can change your life is you. Are you putting up your own barriers?

Do

Write yourself a letter dated twelve months from now. This letter should begin with 'Dear [Your name here]' and detail precisely how you achieved a goal that you currently have – all in the past tense. At the end, you'll have a rough map for focusing on the things in your life that are in your hands. This ingenious method is called the Zander Letter, after the conductor and music professor who developed it, Benjamin Zander. It encourages us to ignore the things we can't influence and to instead focus on the things we can.

Date:
Dear

_____

_____

_____

_____

_____

_____

_____

_____

_____

_____

Yours,

Inspire

'A lot of times I would lose the game and I would sleep soundly . . . because I knew that I put every single ounce of me into trying to be successful.'

Osi Umenyiora, former NFL player and two-time Super Bowl winner

Think

Listening to other people's criticisms and reacting negatively can lead to poor performance. Trying to bring about such poor performance in other people is known as 'sledging', a tactic perfected by the Australian national cricket team in the 1990s, who would aim for what captain Steve Waugh called the 'mental disintegration of opponents' before a single ball was even bowled.

All too often, we sledge *ourselves* – by focusing on what we can't do at the expense of what we can. Think about a time you've talked yourself down. Did it lead to better or worse performance?

_____

_____

_____

_____

_____

_____

Do

Reflect on three areas of your life. They could be work, home, sport – anything. Now, ask yourself, 'What can I control in this part of my life?'

1. _____

_____

_____

2. _____

_____

_____

3. _____

_____

_____

FOCUS ON THE PROBLEM
AT HAND

Last week's focus was **what can you control?** We learned how high performers always focus on the areas of their life that are in their hands. What did you learn?

_____

_____

_____

Think about your **goals** for the year. What have you done in the past week to help you achieve them?

_____

_____

_____

This week's theme is **focus on the problem at hand.** High performers never overgeneralise – they just focus on the issue in front of them. What does focusing on the problem at hand mean to you?

_____

_____

_____

Think

All too often, when we encounter a problem, we overgeneralise. As a result, we view a temporary situation through the lens of the three 'Ps' – such that we think of the issue as pervasive, permanent and personal. High performers, on the other hand, consistently notice the exceptions, and search for the upside. They think of problems as specific, temporary and external.

Can you think of moments when you've overgeneralised in the face of a problem? What about when you've managed to look on the bright side?

_____

_____

_____

_____

_____

_____

_____

_____

_____

_____

_____

_____

_____

_____

Inspire

'I feel like I'm taking responsibility by just trying to learn, day by day. If I can become a better coach, it's up to me.'

Frank Lampard, Everton manager and former West Ham, Chelsea and England player

Do

Let's look at those three 'Ps' that indicate you might be over-generalising one by one. The first one is *pervasive*. Think of three general terms that you've used recently ('everybody', 'no one', 'totally', 'completely', 'everything'). Such general terms can be dangerous because they encourage us to make lazy generalisations rather than attempt to gain a deep understanding of an issue.

But there's a solution. When you find yourself thinking, *Everything about this project is going wrong*, try to think of the elements of it (however small) that have gone right. When you spot a friend saying, 'They always do X,' try to offer up an example of when they've done Y. In the space below, write down three moments in your life when a problem has felt 'pervasive' – and how, in the end, you realised it wasn't.

1. _____

2. _____

3. _____

Inspire

'You can have a flat graph when it comes to hearing, and still be a profound listener.'

Evelyn Glennie, the world's premier solo percussionist

Do

The second P is similarly toxic: thinking that a problem is *permanent*. Write down three times you have seen a difficulty as permanent – using words like 'always', 'all the time' or 'never' ('I never get it right,' 'This always happens to me,' 'Every time I try').

1. _____

2. _____

3. _____

This is dangerous. What you are doing is telling others – and, most crucially, yourself – that the problem you have is inescapable rather than short-term. Now, rewrite those three examples using words or phrases like 'occasionally', 'recently', 'lately' and 'some of the time', which are far more empowering.

1. _____

2. _____

3. _____

Think

The third P is *personal*. In the space below, write down something that has gone wrong. Did you turn the focus of failure upon yourself? ('How could I have been so stupid?') When you immediately start to turn the focus inwards and blame yourself for the problem, you are making it personal – and it is rarely helpful.

_____

_____

_____

_____

_____

_____

_____

_____

_____

_____

_____

_____

_____

_____

_____

_____

OWNING YOUR MISTAKES

Last week's theme was **focus on the problem at hand**. We looked at the dangers of using the three 'Ps' (pervasive, permanent and personal) to overgeneralise. What did you learn?

_____

_____

_____

Think about your **goals** for the year. What have you done in the past week to help you achieve them?

_____

_____

_____

This week's focus is **owning your mistakes**. High performers always own up when they make mistakes rather than looking for someone else to criticise. What does owning your mistakes mean to you?

_____

_____

_____

Inspire

'Humility is one of the fundamentals.'

Anthony Taylor, Premier League referee

Think

A central part of the gruelling training for the Royal Marines is observing people's reaction when things go wrong. The recruiters call this 'dislocation of expectation'. The goal is to take someone and throw them headlong out of their comfort zone, then see how they respond. The Marines believe that, under stress, a person's natural state comes to the surface. How do you react under pressure? Do you focus on the problem before you, or do you look round for someone to blame?

_____

_____

_____

_____

_____

_____

_____

_____

_____

Do

When we don't own up to our mistakes, we are prone to repeat them – we can't learn the lessons we need to unless we accept that we've done wrong. For this reason, one mistake can easily cascade into more mistakes – and then more, and more and more.

At the top of the below diagram, write down a mistake you've made in the past. In the next box write down the next mistake it led to, and so on. Now think: if you'd owned up in the first place, would the second and third mistakes have happened?

Mistake 1:

Mistake 2:

Mistake 3:

Inspire

'There's a fear of being wrong. And that fear, especially in our society, is debilitating: fear of ridicule, fear of what people might think, fear of failure, whatever ... But for me, the biggest failure is not trying.'

*Chrissie Wellington, four-time Ironman
triathlon world champion*

Do

In the exercise on the previous page you listed three mistakes. Let's revisit one of those mistakes – but this time, think about what you learned from it. Did the mistake lead you to behave differently thereafter? Write down your learnings in the cloud below. As we all know, every cloud has a silver lining. No mistake is ever just a mistake – it's a chance to learn, grow and become a better you.

Think

Ant Middleton went to prison for assault. He later described the fight he had and the ensuing sentence as 'probably one of the best things that ever happened', because it gave him the wake-up call that inspired him to become a success in the worlds of television, publishing and live theatre. I've seen this principle described as being 'flawsome': just because we're flawed doesn't mean we're not awesome. Do you know anyone who has made a high-profile mistake, owned it and emerged as a better person?

_____

_____

_____

_____

_____

_____

_____

_____

_____

_____

_____

_____

_____

_____

LESSON IN REVIEW
RESPONSIBILITY

This lesson was about **responsibility**. We explored focusing on what we can control, dealing with the problem at hand and the importance of owning your mistakes. What did you learn?

_____

_____

_____

Think about your **goals** for the year. What have you done in the past week to help you achieve them?

_____

_____

_____

This week we're going to summarise what we've learnt about **responsibility**. Has this lesson made you see it differently?

_____

_____

_____

_____

Inspire

'When you're in tough situations, the last thing you should do is do what everybody else is doing.'

Steve Morgan, businessman and philanthropist

Think

By now, you should be able to make out some features of a high-performance worldview. High performers take absolute responsibility for their actions. They focus on the elements of their life that they can control, they avoid overgeneralising in tough situations, and they own up when they mess up. We can summarise this worldview in a simple equation:

$$L + R = O$$
(Life + Response = Outcome)

In the space below, reflect on what you've learnt about high performance in this lesson. Do you feel you can apply this responsibility equation to your own life?

_____

_____

_____

_____

_____

_____

Do

Think about three recent experiences that were either disappointments or great successes. Now, write down how each one can be explained through the responsibility equation. Do you put more emphasis on the 'L' or the 'R'?

High performers tend to focus on the second part of the equation. If you don't like the outcomes you're getting, it's all too easy to focus on the 'Life' component – the things you can't affect – but where does that leave you? On the other hand, you can emphasise the 'Response' part of the equation. Think about what you *can* change: your mindset, your language, your behaviour. High performance is in your hands.

Life	+	Response	=	Outcome

Inspire

'The only limits you ever impose on yourself, come from yourself. You are your own limit.'

John McAvoy, Ironman champion and former criminal

Do

On the podcast, the legendary striker Robin van Persie described coming to an agreement with his son following an under-14s football match. After spending the whole ninety minutes on the bench, his son was complaining about everyone apart from himself. Van Persie's response was simple: the only person who loses out when you think like this is *you*. They agreed there and then on the solution: in future, his son would take 100 per cent responsibility for himself. In the box below, write a similar contract with the future you. Use the insights from this chapter to explore why responsibility is so crucial and make an agreement with yourself that, from now on, you'll take ownership of your life.

Responsibility Contract
Signed: Date:

Lesson round-up

Taking complete responsibility for yourself is the first step to high performance. No one can control what happens to them, but everyone can control their response.

There are three steps to taking responsibility for your life:

1. Isolate the elements of your situation that you can control, and focus your time and attention on them.
2. Focus on the issue at hand, and don't overgeneralise. Try to think about what you can do about the problem that is in front of you.
3. Accept responsibility when you screw up – as all of us do, all the time.

Remember what Robin van Persie said: 'Losers look for blame, winners look to themselves.' We can move towards high performance only by focusing on our own actions.

SELF-TALK

Simone Biles is the greatest gymnast of her generation. By her mid-twenties, she had already won seven Olympic medals, become a seven-time all-round US national champion and been named one of *Time* magazine's 100 most influential people in the world. But her greatest legacy may not be her trophy cabinet, but her powerful advocacy on the importance of mental health.

Biles has spoken openly about the noise in her head every time she steps out on a competition mat. In her book *Courage to Soar*, Biles explains how she keeps calm under pressure. 'You have this,' she tells herself before she begins every routine. It's a prime example of what we call 'positive self-talk'.

According to the Mayo Clinic, a medical research centre based in the USA, self-talk is 'the endless stream of unspoken thoughts that run through your head'. It can be positive ('You have this') or negative ('You can't do it'). On the podcast, we've heard time and again about how high performers – whether athletes, coaches or businesspeople – use self-talk to get themselves into the 'zone' or to calm their nerves before an important event.

This might sound fanciful: surely there's no way that something as mundane as saying 'You have this' can transform your performance? But the science is clear: self-talk works. In one systematic study from 2011, David Tod of the University of Aberystwyth and his colleagues found that positive self-talk has a strong beneficial effect on sportspeople's performance.

So, self-talk matters – and the good news is that anyone can master it. Here, we'll explore how to ensure our self-talk is positive, easy-to-remember and useful.

Reflections:

_____

_____

_____

_____

_____

_____

_____

_____

_____

_____

_____

_____

_____

_____

_____

_____

Inspire

'What no one could take away from me was self-belief.'

Nims Purja, mountaineer

Think

We all have self-talk running through our heads all day: 'You're doing great,' 'That was annoying,' 'It's all going wrong.' Sometimes it's clear, sometimes it's confused, sometimes it's flippant: the England and Lancashire cricketer Jos Buttler has 'Fuck it' written on his bat, to remind himself to keep cool. But whatever form it takes, self-talk is always there. What are the things you say to yourself from day to day? Do you think you tend towards positive or negative self-talk?

_____

_____

_____

_____

_____

_____

_____

_____

Inspire

'Don't ever leave the bathroom without high-fiving the human being you see in the mirror.'

Mel Robbins, bestselling author and motivational speaker

Do

It is surprisingly easy to turn negative self-talk into positive self-talk. One powerful 2014 study from the University of Michigan hints at how: simply changing the things you say to yourself from the first person ('I am') to the second ('You are') miraculously makes your self-talk more likely to be positive. Suddenly, 'I can't do this' becomes 'You can do this.' Look at the examples in the below table – and use the spaces to reflect on when in your day you might use each phrase. How will you integrate positive self-talk into your life?

Negative 'I'	Positive 'You'
'I can't do this'	'You can try this – nothing ventured, nothing gained'
'This will never work'	'You can have a go'

Do

The four main types of self-talk are listed in the grid below. Each comes in handy at different times. For example, 'calming' self-talk helps most when you're feeling stressed, whereas 'instructional' self-talk is most useful in the midst of high-skill tasks. In the boxes, write in your own personal mantras for situations you frequently encounter. Remember to keep them in the second person.

Calming Example: 'Take a deep breath'	**Instructional** Example: 'Keep your back straight'
Motivational Example: 'You've got this'	**Focus** Example: 'Concentrate'

Lesson round-up

The post-win self-talk of Daniel Ståhl, the Swedish Olympic discus champion, became a viral sensation in 2021: he shouted, 'I am a Swedish Viking! Aaaaaaah!' But for all the online ridicule, Ståhl's method clearly worked: after all, how many of his Twitter trolls had won an Olympic gold? He was not worried about what anyone else would think – his self-talk was motivational, inspirational and hit the spot. How will you make your mantra as big, wild and loud as it needs to be? Remember: nobody ever feels ridiculous with a gold medal around their neck.

Reflections:

_____

_____

_____

_____

_____

_____

_____

_____

_____

_____

_____

_____

Motivation

INNER MOTIVATION, OUTER MOTIVATION

Last week's focus was **self-talk**. We explored why the things we say to ourselves matter, and how to make them positive, easy-to-remember and useful. What did you learn?

_____

_____

_____

Think about your **goals** for the year. What have you done in the past week to help you achieve them?

_____

_____

_____

This week's focus is **inner motivation, outer motivation**. High performers are rarely motived by external rewards; instead they tend to have a deep sense of inner drive. What does inner motivation mean to you?

_____

_____

_____

Inspire

'Your definition of success has got to come from within – that sense that you have given something everything.'

Chrissie Wellington, four-time Ironman triathlon world champion

Think

You've probably noticed that high performers have an extraordinary sense of drive: they are unrelentingly committed to being their best. But we often get the source of this motivation wrong. It's easy to think that motivation is all about getting the rewards right – that with the right salary or enough prestige, we'll feel driven. The truth is that external rewards can only get you so far – because true motivation comes from within. Psychologists call this 'intrinsic motivation'. Think about your own life. When do you feel intrinsically motivated?

_____

_____

_____

_____

_____

_____

_____

Do

Sports psychologists Graham Jones and Adrian Moorhouse identified the below four categories of motivation in their book *Developing Mental Toughness*. In the box on the right, write down a moment you have experienced each type of motivation in five words or fewer. Do you particularly relate to any one category, or do you relate to certain details from different ones? For most high performers, their drive in their chosen field will sit in those last two rows – in other words, they have internal motivation.

Category	Definition	Me
Complete non-self-determined	You work hard because you need external rewards to feel OK.	
Low self-determined	You work hard because you like to be rewarded for your success, and these rewards are integrated into your sense of self-worth.	
High self-determined	You work hard because you enjoy the act itself. Success gives you a sense of satisfaction, allowing you to do more of the things you enjoy.	
Complete self-determined	You work hard because you love it. Taking part is all that matters, and external rewards don't feature. You can even forget such rewards exist.	

Inspire

'Sometimes I would stop on the drive home from [training ground] Melwood and just sit in the car and tell myself, "I'm captain of Liverpool Football Club."'

Steven Gerrard, Aston Villa manager and former Liverpool and England footballer

Do

In the grid below, plot four or five of the different tasks that you encounter in your day-to-day life. Include things you do both for money and for fun, ranging from the dullest admin tasks to your most beloved hobbies. Can you see a pattern emerging? For many people, this is the quickest way to show the power of internal motivation. The things you enjoy – that is, tasks you find internally motivating – tend to be the ones you excel at. Internal motivation gets results.

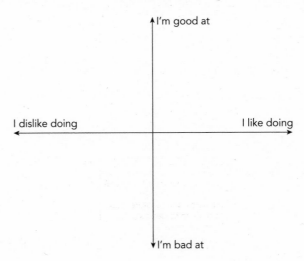

Think

The CrossFit athlete Zack George found that external rewards for losing weight only led to short-term success. A shift in mindset caused Zack to realise that doing things for himself was all the motivation he needed. In common with many high performers, what was driving him to greatness came from within. Think about a reward you were offered for completing a task. Did it lead you to feel more or less motivated, in both the short term and the long term?

BE TRUE TO YOU

Last week's focus was **inner motivation, outer motivation**. We explored why 'intrinsic' drive is so much more powerful than external rewards. What did you learn?

_____

_____

_____

Think about your **goals** for the year. What have you done in the past week to help you achieve them?

_____

_____

_____

This week's focus is **be true to you**. Psychologists say there are three drivers of internal motivation: the first is 'autonomy', or acting in harmony with your true sense of self. What does being true to yourself mean to you?

_____

_____

_____

_____

Think

According to the psychologist Sara James, when our job is in harmony with our sense of self, 'Work provides answers to [an individual's] fundamental questions: "Who am I?" and "What should I do with my life?"' This sense of internal harmony is called 'autonomy' – and is the only way to make sure that *what we do* truly chimes with *who we are*. In what moments do you feel like you are acting in harmony with who you are?

_____

_____

_____

_____

_____

_____

_____

_____

_____

_____

_____

_____

_____

_____

_____

Inspire

'I didn't need any external reward. I just wanted to be happier, be healthier, and tap into my full potential.'

Zack George, CrossFit athlete and the UK's fittest man

Do

We feel a strong sense of autonomy when we're acting in line with our values. Circle words from the list below that are fundamental to your life (aim for five or six). These could be the forces that give you a strong sense of autonomy – and in turn motivate you.

Courage   *Creativity*   *Commitment*   *Dependability*   *Determination*

Efficiency   *Empathy*   *Loyalty*   *Optimism*   *Passion*

Positivity   *Respect*   *Reliability*   *Self-reliance*   *Teamwork*

Inspire

'If it's not your natural calling, don't force it.'

Reece Wabara, fashion CEO and former Manchester City and England footballer

Think

Think about what you do for work (or how you spend your time during the day). Does your work reflect your true sense of self? If not, why not? For greater motivation, your work should reflect who you are. To be truly motivated, you need to feel able to be yourself.

_____

_____

_____

_____

_____

_____

_____

_____

_____

_____

_____

Do

How can we find these moments of autonomous motivation, in which we're driven by that all-consuming sense that a task is part of who we are? The Venn diagram below might help. In the top circle, write down some of the moments in which you feel most at ease with yourself. In the bottom circle, write down the moments in which you feel you're doing your best and most valuable work. In the middle, write down the moments in which these two feelings overlap. Now think: in these moments, do I feel a strong sense of autonomy?

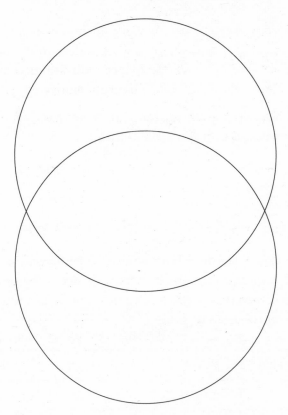

TAKING CONTROL

Last week's focus was **be true to you**. We looked at the power of autonomy, how it relates to our core values, and how it can boost our motivation. What did you learn?

_____

_____

_____

Think about your **goals** for the year. What have you done in the past week to help you achieve them?

_____

_____

_____

This week's focus is **taking control**. The second driver of internal motivation is known as 'competence' – the sense that we have complete control over what we're doing. What does taking control mean to you?

_____

_____

_____

Inspire

'It is all about the controllable elements – the process.'

Tom Daley, World and Olympic diving champion,
LGBT+ activist

Think

Competence refers to our sense of mastery of an area: we believe we are in charge, and that feels good. We can bolster our sense of competence through the very act of making decisions. 'Each choice – no matter how small – reinforces the perception of control and self-efficacy,' a group of psychologists from Columbia and Rutgers universities wrote in 2010. Think about your own life: are there moments when you feel particularly in control, and particularly motivated?

_____

_____

_____

_____

_____

_____

_____

_____

Do

Tom Daley is a strong advocate of taking control of a situation. He writes a list every day of three things he aims to achieve, and focuses on them – instead of the things he can't influence. We can all follow suit. In the outcome box below, write down something you want. In the process box next to it, write down what you can do to help get there. Try to make these actions simple, practical and achievable – in other words, focus on the sort of areas in which you can easily exercise your competence.

Outcome	Process

Inspire

'I know the secret to high performance ... It's realising that there will always be resistance, and there will always be fear.'

Mel Robbins, bestselling author
and motivational speaker

Do

This exercise is based on a process reportedly advocated by Winston Churchill. To start, make two lists with the headings 'Things I can do something about' and 'Things I cannot do anything about'. Churchill is rumoured to have had a rule: 'Do something about the things you can do something about – and then go to sleep.' It's a profound method. If you're ever feeling demotivated, write down all of the things that are in your hands – and cut out everything else.

Things I can do something about:

1. _____

2. _____

3. _____

Things I cannot do anything about:

1. _____

2. _____

3. _____

Think

The legendary rugby coach Gregor Townsend once gave an inspirational talk to the Scottish rugby team. It was half-time, and Scotland were trailing England 31–7, heading for their greatest ever defeat at Twickenham. He told his team to focus on the behaviours they could control: being brave, taking risks and sticking together. The effects were transformative: the team scored five tries in the second half and ultimately tied the game 38–38. It was a valuable lesson in motivation – or rather, demotivation. Think about a time you've been demotivated. What would have gone differently if you'd focused on the things you *could* do?

_____

_____

_____

_____

_____

_____

_____

FINDING WHERE YOU BELONG

Last week's focus was **taking control**. We looked at the power of taking control of a situation, even when things feel hopeless. What did you learn?

_____

_____

_____

Think about your **goals** for the year. What have you done in the past week to help you achieve them?

_____

_____

_____

This week's focus is **finding where you belong**. The third driver of internal motivation is relatedness, which means a sense of belonging. What does finding where you belong mean to you?

_____

_____

_____

_____

Do

Below is your support circle. Inside, write down all the people who you feel support you in achieving your goals. They might be a partner, colleague, friend – even a friendly postman. Add as many people as you can, each offering a different kind of support. Does being around these people enhance your motivation? If so, why?

Think

Frank Lampard was brought into West Ham United when his uncle was the manager and his father a club legend. Many fans thought he wasn't ready. However, thanks in part to the support of his uncle, Lampard proved those fans wrong – and eventually established himself as one of the greatest midfielders of the twenty-first century, first for the Hammers and then at Chelsea. Lampard says that sense of 'East End' belonging helped motivate him to be his best. Have you ever been motivated by a strong sense of belonging?

_____

_____

_____

_____

_____

_____

_____

_____

Inspire

'High performance is a group of people. It's certainly not me as an individual.'

Mary Portas, retail and brand communication expert

Do

In the space below write down three things you have done (or can do) to make people feel they are part of your team. It can be anything: remembering a birthday, sharing a joke, knowing someone's favourite lunch. Even small things can contribute towards a group's sense of direction, purpose and relatedness.

1. _____

2. _____

3. _____

Inspire

'Northampton Saints is more than just a club to me. It has been a place that has provided me with direction, purpose, a sense of family, home and belonging.'

Dylan Hartley, former England rugby and Northampton Saints team captain

Think

One of the greatest ways to build belonging is through other people. Sometimes you need a 'glue guy' to make a team act as one. Eddie Jones, head coach of the England rugby team, spotted that talent in his captain, Dylan Hartley. 'I was interested in his ability to engage positively with different people. It was clear he could bring the players together,' he said. Do you know a 'glue guy' of this kind? What do they do that you admire? What can you learn from them?

_____

_____

_____

_____

_____

_____

_____

_____

_____

_____

_____

_____

_____

_____

_____

LESSON IN REVIEW
MOTIVATION

This lesson was about **motivation**. We learned about the difference between internal and external drive, and the three forces that contribute to lasting motivation. What did you learn?

_____

_____

_____

Think about your **goals** for the year. What have you done in the past week to help you achieve them?

_____

_____

_____

This week we're going to summarise what we've learnt about **motivation**. Has this lesson made you see it differently?

_____

_____

_____

_____

Inspire

'Internal motivation brings a self-confidence and self-happiness that no external award can give you.'

Zack George, CrossFit athlete and the UK's fittest man

Think

As we've seen in this lesson, the secrets to internal motivation lie in a shift in mindset. The first step is to realise that long-term motivation isn't about extrinsic goodies, like a pay rise or gaining followers on Instagram. It's about your own inner drive: the ability to enjoy something on its own terms and feel good about the rewards inherent in doing it. Use this space to reflect on how this insight affects you. Has it changed the way you think about what's driving you?

Do

The most empowering insight into motivation is also the simplest: it's something all of us can build. Provided we're being true to ourselves, exercising control over the things we can control and seeking out environments where we belong, we can build our motivation every day. In the below schedule, add in some of the tasks that make up your average routine – having breakfast, commuting to work, going for a run. List what you can do to build your motivation in each by exercising your autonomy, competence and relatedness.

	My day
Action	
Motivator	

Inspire

'I stumbled across my personal purpose. Through hard work and a lot of sacrifice, my dream became a reality.'

Dan Carter, New Zealand rugby player and highest point scorer in test rugby

Do

There's one powerful feature of internal motivation that we haven't touched upon. We call it the ripple effect. Once you've found intrinsic motivation in one area, it ripples out into the others – such that a strong sense of motivation for one task can gradually spread across your whole life.

The below diagram will help you think through how this works. In the middle circle, write down a time you've felt particularly intrinsically motivated. In the outer two circles, try to pin down the positive effect it had on other areas of your life. Do you find that the more motivated you feel, the easier everything becomes?

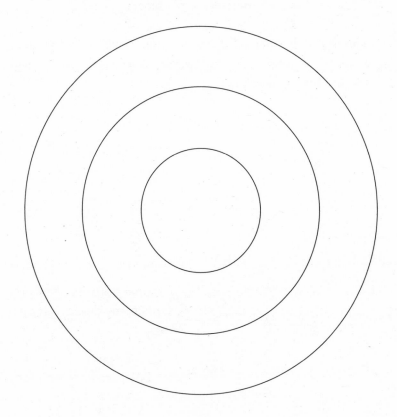

Lesson round-up

While material rewards and social status can drive motivation in the short term, they're rarely enough in the long run. True motivation comes from within.

This internal motivation comes from three sources:

1. Be true to you. When your behaviour aligns with your values, it's easier to get excited about it.
2. Take control. We are most motivated when we have control over what we're doing.
3. Find where you belong. When we feel part of something bigger than ourselves – like a team – we can sustain our motivation for longer.

The value of internal drive goes far beyond motivation, however. It's good for your whole worldview. Motivated people are happy people.

COMMUNICATION

What do you think of when someone mentions Steve Jobs? You might think of his entrepreneurial genius. After all, this was the man who co-founded Apple and revolutionised the market for personal computers not once, but twice – first developing the Apple Mac and then, following a decade outside the company, going on to launch the iPod and iPhone. Or perhaps you think of his visionary creativity. During his time away from Apple, Jobs found time to co-found Pixar – the company behind films such as *Toy Story* and *Monsters, Inc.*

But all this belies Jobs' most remarkable talent: communication. *Forbes* magazine once described him as the 'ultimate communicator'. Clear communication was at the heart of everything Jobs did: whether explaining to the public why they really needed that iPhone, or to investors precisely why they should give Apple their money. By the end of his life, Jobs was widely recognised as the master of the keynote speech.

Listening back to those iconic keynotes, one can start to piece together how he did it. Dressed entirely in black, Jobs would enthral his audience with succinct, interesting and human insights. He rarely resorted to wordy PowerPoint presentations loaded with numbers and graphs. Instead, he homed in on attention-grabbing messages: 'Think different', 'Stay hungry, stay foolish', 'Here's to the crazy ones'. And during his presentations, he walked the stage freely, never preaching from behind a lectern.

Jobs' life offers some powerful insights into the power of good communication. Fortunately, it's a skill that anyone can learn. In this chapter, we'll draw on Jobs' example to explore the key skills you need to get your message across.

Reflections:

_____

_____

_____

_____

_____

_____

_____

_____

_____

_____

_____

_____

_____

_____

_____

_____

_____

_____

Do

Ask three people you trust what they think of your communication style. Ask them to comment on your body language, your word choice and your use of storytelling. Do they think you communicate effectively? What do you do well, and what could you do differently?

_____'s feedback on how I communicate:

_____

_____

_____

_____

_____

_____'s feedback on how I communicate:

_____

_____

_____

_____

_____

_____'s feedback on how I communicate:

_____

_____

_____

_____

_____

Inspire

'You can't lay down laws and then just stand back and watch . . . You have to speak to the players, change it, ask why, what do they think about it, and get close to them.'

Frank Lampard, Everton manager and former West Ham, Chelsea and England player

Think

Not everyone's communication skills are as good as Steve Jobs' – not yet, anyway. But most of us have encountered people who have an innate knack for getting their message across. Think of the most effective communicator you know. What makes them so articulate and compelling?

Think

Communication is about more than merely talking. Listening is crucial too. If you don't know what the people around you are feeling, then you won't know how to get your message across. Take a moment to think about 'active listening'. The United States Institute of Peace describes this as 'a way of listening and responding to another person that improves mutual understanding'. Do you think you are an active listener?

_____

_____

_____

_____

_____

_____

_____

_____

_____

_____

_____

_____

_____

_____

Do

We all have to explain things all the time – to our bosses, clients, partners, children. But all too often we launch straight into our explanations without thinking through how to get our message across. This exercise will help you hone your explanation skills. Try to succinctly explain the below concepts to the following tricky audiences – and remember to keep your explanations succinct, jargon-free and entertaining.

Premier League football . . . to a six-year-old
Instagram . . . to an octogenarian grandmother
Why you need a pay rise . . . to your boss's boss's boss

Lesson round-up

So, what can we all learn from Steve Jobs' communication style? Well, a few things. First, simplicity: he cut out the big numbers and complex jargon when he gave a presentation, which meant he could communicate his points to millions of people. Second, clarity: he knew his subject matter, and precisely the idea he wanted to get across. And third, preparation: he rehearsed endlessly, leading to polished, compelling performances. These are insights we can all use. If you draw upon them, you might not necessarily launch a $3 trillion company (although who knows?), but you'll certainly be able to land your message with aplomb.

Reflections:

_____

_____

_____

_____

_____

_____

_____

_____

_____

_____

_____

Calm

MONITORING YOUR EMOTIONS

Last week's focus was **communication**. We examined how to communicate clearly, eloquently and succinctly. What did you learn?

_____

_____

_____

Think about your **goals** for the year. What have you done in the past week to help you achieve them?

_____

_____

_____

This week's focus is **monitoring your emotions**. We are going to think about how we react under pressure, and how it relates to our performance. What does monitoring your emotions mean to you?

_____

_____

_____

_____

Think

Nobel Prize-winning biologist James Watson once described the human brain as 'the most complex thing we have yet discovered in our universe'. This almighty organ makes an almighty fuss when the shit is about to hit the fan – or when it *thinks* the shit is about to hit the fan. We experience this fuss in the form of stress. Use this space to reflect on stress and how you react to it. Do you find it easy to keep a clear head?

_____

_____

_____

_____

_____

_____

_____

_____

_____

Inspire

'You need adrenaline to gear up for a race, but too much and you are lost.'

Kelly Holmes, Olympic and Commonwealth running champion

Do

The options below represent your brain's default responses to a high-pressure situation. Think of stressful moments from your life and reflect on whether your reaction fitted one of the categories. Write your answers around the three ovals. What does this tell you about your usual response to pressure?

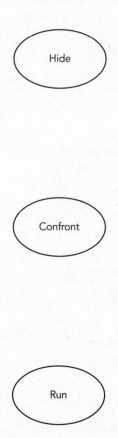

Inspire

'Your emotional brain is neither good nor bad. It fulfils essential functions, but it is also powerful – and prone to panic.'

Chris Hoy, six-time Olympic gold-winning cyclist

Think

It is possible to get our noisy brains under control. Many high performers have models to employ when confronted with emotional problems. A personal favourite comes from the New Zealand rugby team, who worked with world-renowned psychiatrist Ceri Evans. He talks about the emotional, impulsive part of our minds as the 'red brain', and the conscious, rational part of our minds as the 'blue brain'. In moments of extreme pressure, you want your blue brain to be firmly in the driver's seat. Do you have any tricks to keep your red brain in check?

Do

An important step in controlling your emotions is learning to spot when your red brain has become too dominant. Think of your reaction the last time you were confronted with a problem. Now ask yourself the following question: 'If I were looking at this situation from the outside, would I think that reaction is helpful?' Write your answer in the 'verdict' section below. Employing this question will allow you to get outside yourself and assess whether your stress response is as helpful as it could be.

The problem:

_____

_____

_____

_____

↓

The reaction:

_____

_____

_____

_____

↓

The verdict:

_____

_____

_____

_____

WHAT IS DEMANDED OF ME?

Last week's focus was **monitoring your emotions**. We looked at how our judgement can be clouded if we allow our emotional red brain to get out of control. What did you learn?

_____

_____

_____

Think about your **goals** for the year. What have you done in the past week to help you achieve them?

_____

_____

_____

This week's focus is **what is demanded of me?** The first way to avoid panicking under pressure is to develop a clear sense of the actual task before you. What does this idea mean to you?

_____

_____

_____

_____

Inspire

'Fear is a really motivating force, if you don't approach it as fear – but as something that gets you to do the thing you need to do.'

Angela Ruggiero, four-time Olympic ice hockey medallist

Think

When we find a problem stressful, it's tempting to simply not think about it. This was the method used by Olympic cyclist Chris Hoy, at least. The problem with this approach, he told us, related to elephants. He recalled a conversation with his coach, Steve Peters, who asked him how he'd respond if someone broke the world record just before he was due to get on the track. 'I replied, "Well, I just won't think about it,"' Hoy recalled. '"Don't think about a pink elephant," Peters instructed. What was the first thing that pops into my head? A pink elephant!' The lesson, Hoy told us, is that the best way to overcome a daunting situation is to think about it in detail – by thinking, *What is actually demanded of me?* Try this with a stressful situation from your own life. Does this question make it less daunting?

Do

This 'pink elephant method' is all about focusing on the specific, small steps you can take to overcome a stressful situation. In the left-hand column, write down a task you find challenging or difficult. In the right-hand column, write down the specific steps you need to take to tackle that task. The goal is to think rationally, not emotionally, about what you're facing.

The challenge	What is required of me?
	1.
	2.
	3.

Inspire

'If you want to eat an elephant, you've got to do it piece by piece.'

Christian Horner, team principal of Red Bull F1 and winner of nine world titles

87

Do

As Christian Horner's quote indicates, one useful way to make a daunting task manageable is to divide it into stages. When a task feels too demanding, that's often because you haven't thought through what it actually entails, step by step. In the below diagram, identify the small steps you can take to overcome a problem in your life – the smaller the pieces of elephant, the better.

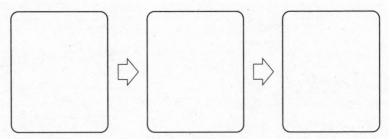

Think

Chris Hoy used all these insights to great effect in the 2012 Olympics. By visualising the task before him, and breaking it into manageable chunks, he was able to turn a terrifying moment into something he could handle – along the way breaking a world record. Think back through your life. When did you last find a task wasn't as difficult as you expected – and what did you learn from that experience?

WHAT ARE MY ABILITIES?

Last week's focus was **what is demanded of me?** We learned to focus on what each of us can do to overcome a stressful situation. What did you learn?

_____

_____

_____

Think about your **goals** for the year. What have you done in the past week to help you achieve them?

_____

_____

_____

This week's focus is **what are my abilities?** If the first step to managing stress is focusing on what is _actually_ demanded of you, the second step is even simpler: identify the skills you _do_ have to overcome the problem. What does this idea mean to you?

_____

_____

_____

Inspire

'My coach reminded me that what I already had within me was what I needed to win.'

Dina Asher-Smith, record-breaking sprinter

Think

On the podcast, Dina Asher-Smith told us how she overcame the tendency to panic by focusing on the abilities she *did* have. It's a method she learned from her coach, John Blackie. She described a disappointing race at the 2019 World Athletics Championships, after which she started to panic. 'What are we going to do? she asked. Blackie remained unfazed, his voice calm and even. 'Just go there and do the normal start you have done thousands of times before,' he said. We can all learn from this method. When you feel under pressure, remind yourself of the skills you already have to get you through. What abilities should you have at the forefront of your mind in moments of stress?

Do

Most of the time, we already have the skills we need to over-come a stressful situation, but in moments of panic it's all too easy to forget these skills. One way round this is the 'confidence piggy bank'. Every time you achieve something, try to recall in detail how you achieved it: how you were feeling, what you were thinking, how you behaved. Try it below: in the piggy bank, write down the skill you used to overcome a tricky situation in the past. Becoming actively aware of the qualities that have got you to where you are is like depositing money in the bank. The more you do so, the healthier your balance will be.

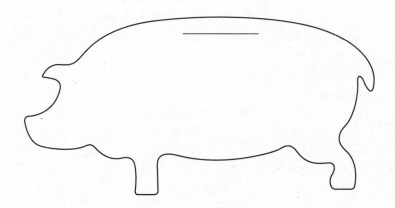

Think

Asher-Smith told us that her relationship with Blackie worked so well because he knew all her abilities inside out. 'I know, hand on heart, that he wouldn't let me do anything or he wouldn't put me in a position that I didn't have the ability to handle,' she said. Is there anyone who plays a similar role in your life, reminding you of the skills you already have?

_____

_____

_____

_____

_____

_____

_____

_____

_____

_____

Inspire

'You explore everything. And if you're exploring, you're going to find something new.'

Jonny Wilkinson, World Cup-winning former England rugby player

Do

Try to build up a mental list of your greatest abilities – the things that your peers always tell you that you excel at. That way, when things get stressful, it's easy to remember which of your skills might get you out of the situation. Write the abilities you uncover inside the stars.

WHAT IS REALLY AT STAKE?

Last week's focus was **what are my abilities?** We learned to focus on the skills we do have when we encounter moments of stress. What did you learn?

_____

_____

_____

Think about your **goals** for the year. What have you done in the past week to help you achieve them?

_____

_____

_____

This week's focus is **what is really at stake?** The final step to managing stress is to focus on the actual consequences if things _did_ go wrong; they are rarely as disastrous as we tend to imagine. What does this idea mean to you?

_____

_____

_____

Inspire

'Results are just an outcome. They are not your worth.'

Pippa Grange, former head of people and team development at the Football Association and advisor to the England football team

Think

On the podcast, rugby legend Jonny Wilkinson explained how the desire not just for success but for perfection would take a huge mental toll on him. His story reveals some crucial insights into the risks of obsessing too much about success and failure. It's all too easy to develop an exaggerated sense of the *consequences* of a stressful situation. But knowing what's actually at stake will help you keep your sense of perspective and remain calm. Do you tend to overestimate the significance of stressful moments?

_____

_____

_____

_____

_____

_____

Do

Very few stressful situations have genuinely ruinous consequences – as this exercise will show. Write down something you deem a failure on the left. In the middle, list any consequences you remember. Finally, write down what you learned, or what you did differently afterwards, on the right. Was the outcome really as momentous as you'd expected?

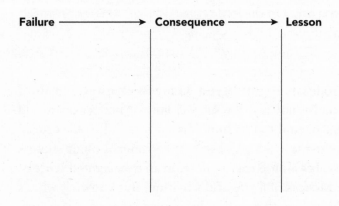

Failure ⟶ Consequence ⟶ Lesson

Inspire

'I learned to let go. I let go of old ideas about who I am and what I had to do.'

Jonny Wilkinson, World Cup-winning former England rugby player

Do

The reason Jonny Wilkinson got so stressed, he told us, was that he struggled to disentangle his professional success from his sense of who he was. Every bump in the road became an existential problem – because it wasn't just a professional issue, but a slight to his innermost self. 'If I *do* this, it means I *am* this. If I *do* that, it means I *am* that,' he put it. It's a toxic cycle. Use the below space to draw a line between what you do and who you are. On the left, write down all the things you're striving for in your high-performance journey. On the right, write down the things that you like about yourself – and that don't depend on accolades or professional success. Remember, the two are not the same: your value does not relate to your performance.

I do . . .   **I am . . .**

Think

When you encounter a stressful situation and start to catastrophise, it can help to speak to someone you trust – and who can tell you the consequences aren't as severe as you think. Is there anyone who always makes you feel calm when you're stressed?

_____

_____

_____

_____

_____

_____

_____

_____

_____

_____

_____

_____

_____

_____

_____

_____

LESSON IN REVIEW
CALM

This lesson was about **calm**. We explored how the brain responds to pressure – with a particular focus on the distinction between your emotional brain and your rational brain: and how to get the former under the control of the latter. What did you learn?

_____

_____

_____

Think about your **goals** for the year. What have you done in the past week to help you achieve them?

_____

_____

_____

This week we're going to summarise what we've learnt about **calm**. Has this lesson made you see it differently?

_____

_____

_____

Think

Even the world's highest-performing people have moments of panic – moments of crisis. Yet all these high performers have something in common: they have developed mechanisms that allow them to get their red brain under wraps, and use these mechanisms to remain in control. Use this space to reflect on what methods you will use to do the same. Revisit the exercises in this chapter as often as you need to – the road may be long, but you are on your way.

Inspire

'You've got to be cool, calm and collected . . . That goes for everything, every walk of life.'

Michael Bisping, Ultimate Fighting Championship Hall of Fame inductee

Do

Getting your red brain in check involves discipline – knowing what's going on in your mind in the moments when you feel the pressure rising, and actively practising keeping a cool head. The road to high performance is long. You don't need to get there right away, and even if you fail, you'll have chances in the future to succeed.

In the footpath below, trace the steps in your road to calm so far. What have been the key breakthroughs and setbacks? What do you think lies ahead?

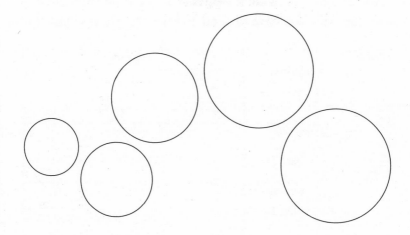

Inspire

'Winning is everywhere ... but we need to be careful not to fall into the trap of finding "winning" as something very narrow, short-term, short-lived and defined by others.'

Cath Bishop, multiple Olympic medallist and business coach

Do

By now, you should have a three-part framework for understanding your red brain. When you start to panic, it's down to the interaction of three factors. There are the **demands** – namely the misconception that the task before you is impossible. There are your **abilities** – in particular, the sense that yours aren't enough. And there are the **consequences** – all too often, an overblown sense of what is at stake.

In the grid below, reflect on how this three-part framework could help you get a more balanced view of a stressful situation. What can you do to get a clearer sense of what is required of you, the skills you have to hand and the actual consequences?

Problem		Solution
	Demands	
	Abilities	
	Consequences	

Lesson round-up

The human brain is prone to panic – but it doesn't have to be. We can prevent our emotional red brain from overpowering our rational blue brain.

But how? When a situation feels overwhelming, first work out what is actually required of you. Take a deep breath and:

1. Reflect on what is demanded of you. Is this really as hard as you're making it out to be?
2. Remind yourself of your abilities. What skills do you have to solve this problem? How have they come in handy before?
3. Reflect on what is at stake. How much does this really matter? Is the worst-case scenario as bad as you think?

These methods take practice, but don't lose hope. The road to inner calm is long, but with time you'll reach its end.

BALANCE

When Naomi Osaka won her second Australian Open in 2021, she cemented her position as one of the world's greatest tennis players – one of only three modern-era players to win their first four Grand Slam finals. But Osaka's track record wasn't the only remarkable feature of her career. Where many of her peers seek out the limelight, Osaka has often rejected interviews with the press. And where many famous tennis players hype themselves up as super-human athletes, Osaka has always emphasised the ordinariness of her life. 'Tennis is my job, similar to how a normal person has a 9-to-5,' she once said. 'When I'm off the court, everything relaxes, and I don't really care that much about what I do or what I say.' In September 2021, Osaka decided to take a break from tennis to focus on her mental health.

Osaka's career offers a profound insight into the power of balance. Rather than give everything over to tennis and ignore all other aspects of her life – a recipe for burnout – Osaka has always prioritised her physical and mental wellbeing. It's an approach we can all learn from. In your journey to high performance, there'll be moments when it feels like everything is getting too much. In these moments, it's imperative that you remember that high performance is only one part of your life: you need to keep making time for your health, your family and your social life. High performance isn't everything.

But what does a healthy approach to balance entail? Part of the answer is simply knowing when to stop. According to one study from the University of Warwick, the simple act of taking a break can help improve productivity by up to 10 per cent. Part of the answer is about discipline, making sure that you're not working past the hours you've decided to give over to a task. This week we'll touch on these insights and more, to help you develop a balanced approach to high performance.

Reflections:

_____

_____

_____

_____

_____

_____

_____

_____

_____

_____

_____

_____

_____

_____

_____

_____

Think

Have there been times when you've struggled to find the right balance – between work and rest, or family and career? Use the space below to reflect on examples of when you were unable to keep the balance right, and how it made you feel.

_____

_____

_____

_____

_____

_____

_____

_____

_____

_____

Inspire

'High performance: it's not just grafting all the time but understanding when you need to rest, when you need to step back.'

Grace Beverley, entrepreneur, CEO and
bestselling author

Do

Balance is all about planning. If you decide beforehand how much work, play and rest you are going to fit into your week – and actually stick to it – then you'll always be getting the balance right. In the space below, succinctly write in the tasks that make up your ideal week. How much time will you give over to work, play and rest? Are there ways to force yourself to stick to this routine?

	Work *I will . . .*	**Play** *I will . . .*	**Rest** *I will . . .*
Sunday			
Monday			
Tuesday			
Wednesday			
Thursday			
Friday			
Saturday			

Think

When you start a big new project, it's easy to feel overwhelmed – like there's no way to even begin. In moments like these, it's easy to overlook the basics: taking breaks, stopping on time and looking after yourself. Use the space below to reflect on the first things you let slip when you encounter pressure. Are there methods you could use to build a more balanced approach?

_____

_____

_____

_____

_____

_____

_____

_____

Inspire

'Don't wait until you're older to retire. Have many retirements every year.'

Joe Wicks, fitness coach, presenter, influencer and bestselling author

Lesson round-up

Life is like a jigsaw made up of a thousand pieces. When you're focusing on only one part of the picture, it seems easy to make everything fit together – but when you look at the whole thing, it can become overwhelming. This week we've learnt how a balanced approach can prevent life feeling like too much. We can all learn from Naomi Osaka's approach. Allow yourself to rest. Forgive yourself. And remember that becoming a high performer is only one part of the puzzle that makes up the human experience.

Reflections:

_____

_____

_____

_____

_____

_____

_____

_____

_____

_____

_____

Strengths

IDENTIFYING YOUR STRENGTHS

Last week's focus was **balance**. We explored why it's important to develop a sustainable approach to high performance, taking rests and not overexerting yourself. What did you learn?

_____

_____

_____

Think about your **goals** for the year. What have you done in the past week to help you achieve them?

_____

_____

_____

This week's focus is **identifying your strengths**. We'll argue that high performers never fixate on what they're bad at – instead, they focus obsessively on what they're great at. What does finding your strengths mean to you?

_____

_____

_____

Inspire

'I'm a firm believer that every individual has the opportunity to be the best in the world at something.'

Ben Francis, entrepreneur and founder of Gymshark

Think

Here's a situation that many parents will find familiar. Imagine your child has come home with a school report card. They show you the following grades:

English: A. Social studies: A. Biology: C. Algebra: F. Maths: C. French: B

Is there a grade that immediately jumps out at you? The polling company Gallup once investigated this very issue. Researchers set out to examine how much parents focus on their children's best grades rather than their worst. The results were striking, revealing that most parents in nearly every country studied immediately focused on the 'F'. The moral was simple: people tend to focus on the negatives. As we'll learn over the next few reflections, this way of thinking can cause us needless trouble. Can you think of a moment when you've focused on the downside of a situation and neglected the upside?

_____

_____

_____

_____

Do

Howard Gardner, a pioneering developmental psychologist, developed a theory about the nature of skill and intelligence. There's not just one form of intellect, he argued, but many. In some scenarios, your particular brand of intelligence might be helpful; in others, it might be useless. And that means that, whether you are academic or not, there'll probably be one area in which you're the brightest person in the room.

The below list cites a few different kinds of intelligence. Draw an arrow between each one and the spot on the line where you think it makes the most sense – with the things you're bad at on the left, and the things you're good at on the right. Everyone excels at something. Which one most chimes with your experience?

I'm bad at

⟵————————————————————————————⟶

I'm good at

I'm good at thinking through complex, abstract ideas

I'm good at creative tasks like drawing and music

I'm good at making sense of numbers and spreadsheets

I'm good at expressing myself clearly and compellingly

I'm good at understanding the emotions of the people around me

I'm good at sports and have strong spatial awareness

Inspire

'I would be naive to say I didn't take anything from school. The main thing I took was understanding people and the way they think.'

Steven Bartlett, award-winning entrepreneur and bestselling author

Think

Jo Malone left school in her early teens to care for her mother. She would go on to create one of the world's best-known perfume brands. 'I always believed that there was something else out there,' she told us on the podcast. Some of our high performers left school with perfect grades, but others dropped out with no formal qualifications. Their 'qualifications' came in a different form. Take this opportunity to think about what qualifications you have, whether academic or otherwise. Finding your strengths does not mean finding a piece of paper.

_____

_____

_____

_____

_____

_____

_____

_____

Do

Reflect on the types of intelligence we discussed below, and use them to identify specific skills you're good at. These can be 'soft' people-based skills or 'hard' practical ones. What matters is that they're areas in which you excel. Don't fixate on what you're bad at. All that matters is what you're great at.

I am fairly good at: _____

_____

_____

_____

I am very good at: _____

_____

_____

_____

I am great at: _____

_____

_____

_____

I am excellent at: _____

_____

_____

_____

GOLDEN SEEDS

Last week's focus was **identifying your strengths**. We looked at the different types of intelligence and helped you to identify yours. What did you learn?

_____

_____

_____

Think about your **goals** for the year. What have you done in the past week to help you achieve them?

_____

_____

_____

This week's focus is **golden seeds**. Sigmund Freud coined this term to refer to early childhood experiences of praise, which he claimed can be an essential part of working out what your strengths are. What does this concept mean to you?

_____

_____

_____

Think

Everyone's journey is different, but many high-performance individuals have overcome problems and triumphed in the face of adversity. Often, they have been inspired by a family member, teacher or friend. Think about who has inspired you, and how they did it. How did they help you find your strengths?

_____

_____

_____

_____

_____

_____

_____

_____

Inspire

'People often credit inspirational teachers they have had at school, those who fired them with enthusiasm for a subject in a way that influenced the rest of their life. For me, that person was Debbie Page.'

Kelly Holmes, Olympic and Commonwealth running champion

Do

Why do golden-seed moments matter? Well, psychologists have long argued the very act of labelling a behaviour makes us inclined to commit to it. Thus, moments of childhood praise can lead to a pattern of positive behaviour. They could be the first moment you realise what might be your calling.

In the grid below, write down any times you can recall that someone told you that you did something well. It could be a family member, teacher, boss – anyone. Record the praise in the first column and when and from whom the praise was received in the second. Then, in the final column identify and label the skill that was complimented. You may not have thought of it as a golden-seed moment at the time, but what about now?

Praise	Who/when	Skill

Inspire

'The most rewarding aspect of the game – of the job – is to be able to have a chat with someone and feel like you've really reached them.'

Alex Sanderson, former professional rugby player and director of rugby for Sale Sharks

Do

We should all make note of our little victories and the skills we used to achieve them, because the resulting insights can drive us on to further success. In the spaces below, write down your recent triumphs (however small), and what you did that contributed to them. For example, if you got a promotion at work, maybe it was down to those extra hours you worked. Or maybe that free coffee you were given was a result of your glowing smile.

I achieved: _____ *by:* _____

_____   _____

_____   _____

I achieved: _____ *by:* _____

_____   _____

_____   _____

I achieved: _____ *by:* _____

_____   _____

_____   _____

Think

This week we have looked at how other people have influenced you and made a difference in your life by praising and helping you. Now think about what you do for others. Do you praise your team? Do you believe someone you know could be great at something, but doesn't realise it? Maybe you could plant a golden seed yourself . . .

_____

_____

_____

_____

_____

_____

_____

_____

_____

_____

_____

_____

_____

_____

_____

_____

_____

SUCCESS LEAVES CLUES

Last week's focus was **golden seeds**. We examined how identifying and labelling our skills – particularly in childhood – can plant the seed for later success. What did you learn?

_____

_____

_____

Think about your **goals** for the year. What have you done in the past week to help you achieve them?

_____

_____

_____

This week's focus is **success leaves clues**. A golden seed won't grow by itself, so we'll learn how to notice and nurture the little triumphs that make up our lives. What does success leaves clues mean to you?

_____

_____

_____

Inspire

'My success isn't measured by how many people download the [fitness] app or subscribe. It's more, how many people actually get a benefit from it.'

Joe Wicks, fitness coach, presenter, influencer and bestselling author

Think

High performers are constantly monitoring the areas in which they're excelling, as well as those in which they're underperforming. If you have a natural knack for something, you'll see the evidence for it all around you. We summarise this idea in a simple maxim: success leaves clues. Use this space to reflect on recent clues from your life about what you're great at. What does the evidence suggest is your unique skillset?

_____

_____

_____

_____

_____

_____

_____

_____

Do

It is time for some honest self-reflection. Make two lists in the spaces below, summarising where you excel – and where you don't. Kelly Holmes used this method to identify her biggest weakness and the barriers to her success. Her experience offers a simple lesson: take time to reflect on your skills, and revisit them whenever you encounter a setback. This process should give you a clearer sense of who you are and what makes you unique.

My strengths:

_____

_____

_____

_____

_____

_____

My weaknesses:

_____

_____

_____

_____

_____

_____

Inspire

'As athletes, we're blessed to have constant feedback on our performance. It's been one of my biggest strengths in my crossover into the business world.'

George Kruis, England, Saracens and Panasonic Wild Knights rugby player, and co-founder of fourfive

Do

When we apply for a job, we talk about our greatest strengths with bravado. We usually keep these skills at the forefront of our heads until the moment we leave the interview, then immediately forget about them. But this method – thinking about our skills, labelling them, even boasting about them – is a powerful tool for working out what we're great at.

Use the space below to write down three big achievements from the past year and reflect on the skills that allowed you to pull each one off. Which skills are driving you to high performance?

Achievement 1:

_____

_____

_____

_____

Achievement 2:

_____

_____

_____

_____

Achievement 3:

_____

_____

_____

_____

Think

In the previous exercise we listed different achievements and skills. Now go back and take another look. Is there one broader skill that underpins *all* your accomplishments? Often, a single theme unites everything we're great at – whether it's determination to win, self-discipline or creativity. Remember, success leaves clues. What is the biggest clue your successes offer?

_____

_____

_____

_____

FINDING YOUR FLOW

Last week's focus was **success leaves clues.** We explored how each of us can spot our strengths and integrate them into our high-performance journey. What did you learn?

_____

_____

_____

Think about your **goals** for the year. What have you done in the past week to help you achieve them?

_____

_____

_____

This week's focus is **finding your flow.** We'll argue that our strengths are usually those that bring us 'flow' – that sense of complete immersion and creativity in which hours seem to fly by. What does finding your flow mean to you?

_____

_____

_____

Think

Imagine a pianist performing in a concert. Every part of their body is given over to playing, and they seem overjoyed by the complete focus that it requires. The psychologist Mihaly Csikszentmihalyi called this state 'flow', and claimed that it holds the key to productivity and happiness. Indicators of flow include a relaxed look on your face, slower breathing and a lack of muscular tension in the body. Can you think of a moment when you've been in flow?

_____

_____

_____

_____

_____

_____

_____

_____

Inspire

'I always found my best performances were when I went onto autopilot, committed everything and let it go.'

Steven Gerrard, Aston Villa manager and former
Liverpool and England footballer

Do

Csikszentmihalyi and his researchers developed a method called 'experience sampling', in which they sent a message to a group of experimental subjects eight times a day and asked them to write their answers to several short questions in a booklet.

Use the grid below to record how you feel when doing different tasks through the week, putting a number between 1 and 10 in each of the three boxes on the right. Come back to the questions each day, then at the end of the week take the time to see if any patterns have emerged. Csikszentmihalyi used this approach to identify what brings flow – arguing that high happiness, productivity and relaxation are the key ingredients of true immersion. What does your tracker suggest brings you flow?

Task	Happiness	Productivity	Relaxation
1.			
2.			
3.			

Think

When you start asking people about their mindset in moments of high performance, they often describe a state of flow – even if they aren't familiar with Csikszentmihalyi's research. They talk about being 'in the zone', or not being able to think of anything but the game, or the joy of complete concentration. Do you have any tricks to bring about this state in your own life? What are they?

_____

_____

_____

_____

_____

_____

_____

_____

_____

_____

_____

_____

_____

_____

_____

Do

The circles below represent the three pillars of flow – being challenged, doing your best work, and feeling completely immersed. In the circles, fill in some of the tasks you undertake in your average week and note where the circles overlap. When you've finished, take a look at the middle of the Venn diagram. These are the moments that might just bring you flow. What does this tell you about your skill set?

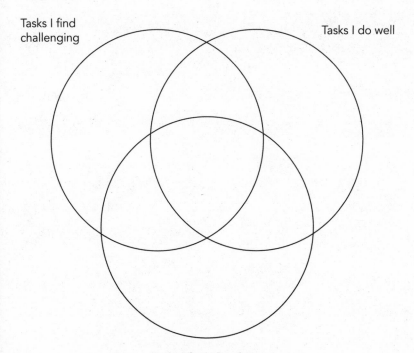

Tasks I find challenging

Tasks I do well

Tasks I find absorbing

Inspire

'All my identity was geared towards playing rugby from early on. When it suddenly gets pulled from under you, it can feel vulnerable ... I had to change myself from within, take responsibility and reflect to nurture my talents.'

*Ollie Phillips, former England rugby sevens captain,
business leader and motivational speaker*

LESSON IN REVIEW
STRENGTHS

Last week's focus was **finding your flow**. We explored why the things you're skilled at may well be those that bring you 'flow' – that all-too-rare sense of total creativity and immersion. What did you learn?

_____

_____

_____

Think about your **goals** for the year. What have you done in the past week to help you achieve them?

_____

_____

_____

This week we're going to summarise what we've learnt about **strengths**. Has this lesson made you see your strengths differently?

_____

_____

_____

Inspire

'I thrive in uncomfortable environments. When I get chucked in, in that moment I feel I can swim.'

Eric Dier, Tottenham Hotspur and England footballer

Think

One of the most important concepts in economics is 'comparative advantage'. It means that everyone in the world gets the best results when they focus on what they're good at. In economic terms, that means if a country has extensive iron reserves, it should focus on exporting iron; if it has lush, fertile land, it should grow crops. By focusing on your strengths, the theory goes, everyone ends up richer.

This month you have thought a lot about identifying your skills and abilities. Now take the opportunity to think about whether you are using them in your daily life. Record how you do play to your strengths – and how you'll change if you don't.

_____

_____

_____

_____

_____

_____

Do

Label the bars in the below bar chart with three of the strengths that you've identified in this lesson. Next, think about how much you use these strengths in your day-to-day life. Colour in the chart accordingly – the more you fill in a bar, the more you're using the skill. If you're playing to your strengths, all three bars should be completely filled in. Is that the case? If not, why not?

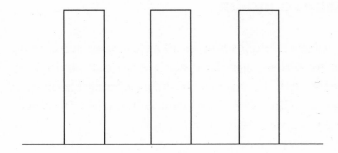

Think

Reflect on the insights in this lesson about finding your strengths. What are the strengths you've discovered that have most surprised you? What will you do today to integrate them into your life?

Inspire

'I'm pretty comfortable knowing what I don't know.'

Dilbagh Gill, CEO and team principal of Mahindra Racing

Lesson round-up

We all have strengths and we all have weaknesses. Yet all too often we obsess over the things we can't do and ignore the things we can. Remember the theory of multiple intelligence: there are myriad ways to be talented. The trick is to find yours. Doing so involves three steps:

1. Think about those instances, perhaps in your youth, when you were told you had a talent. Were they golden-seed moments?
2. Reflect on what you're good at in the here and now. Success leaves clues. It's your job to spot them.
3. Seek out tasks that induce a sense of flow. These moments are rare, but might just reveal your true calling.

Finding these skills is the quickest route to high performance. Each of us can play to our 'comparative advantage' – provided we know how to find it.

FAILURE

Wembley Stadium, 11 July 2021. England vs Italy. This is no regular football match. The final of Euro 2020, the game represents England's first shot at a major international trophy in decades. You can almost taste the excitement in the air: Gareth Southgate's team are playing better than any England squad in years.

As the match against Italy grinds on into extra time and then penalties, the tension at Wembley grows. England's track record at penalties, everyone knows, is abysmal. Will this time be different? At first, everything is going so well: after each side has taken two shots, England is one goal ahead. Then Marcus Rashford steps up to the spot. He misses. When the Italian goalkeeper saves shots from Jadon Sancho and Bukayo Saka, England's hopes of taking home the European title are dashed once more.

Except this time, something is different. In the hours that follow, the country comes alive with praise: for the team culture Southgate built, for the courage of the young England team and for the inspirational achievement of reaching the final. The penalties hiccups are not seen as a failure – they are seen as a story of brave players who stood up and tried their best.

We would all do well to apply this approach to our own lives. Failure is only failure when we interpret it as such. In our podcast interviews, we have learnt that there are three ways to respond to a bump in the road: to give up, to chastise our-selves or to learn the lesson and push on through. On that humid night in 2021, England learned the power of the third way. In this 'In Focus' session we're going to explore failure – or, more aptly, 'failure'. We are all unsuccessful sometimes but, with the right mindset, we can learn to construe these moments not as failures, but as chances to grow.

Reflections:

_____

_____

_____

_____

_____

_____

_____

_____

_____

_____

_____

_____

_____

_____

_____

_____

_____

Inspire

'Flip the mindset to loving when you fail.'

*Angela Ruggiero, four-time Olympic
ice hockey medallist*

Think

How do you generally respond to failure? Use the space below to reflect on whether you tend to give up, chastise yourself or learn a lesson and move on. Do you think your approach is the right one?

_____

_____

_____

_____

_____

_____

_____

_____

_____

_____

Do

Everyone who has known great success will also have known great failure. In fact, their failures are how many high performers got that way. In the inner circle, write what you perceive to be your biggest failure. In the outer circle, write the lessons you learned. Was it really as bad as it felt at the time?

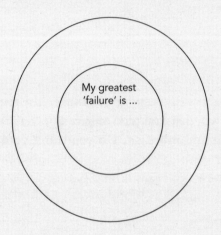

My greatest 'failure' is ...

Think

Angela Duckworth, a psychologist at the University of Pennsylvania, has developed a famous theory about 'grit' – a characteristic she considers the key to success. Grit, she says, is about 'passion and perseverance for very long-term goals'. People with grit push through their failures, sometimes without blinking. Can you think of a time when you have shown grit? What made you able to push through in that situation?

_____

_____

_____

Inspire

'If you're a boxer, I'm pretty sure the hundredth time you're punched in the face it still hurts. Just that time, you're ready for a punch in the face.'

Russell Kane, writer, comedian and actor

Do

Let's return to those three responses to failure: giving up, beating yourself up and pushing through. Let's call them dejection, chastisement and resilience. In the boxes below, write down an example of a time you have responded in each way. Now, think about the consequences of each response. Do you agree that resilience is more constructive than dejection and chastisement? If so, why?

Dejection	Chastisement	Resilience

Lesson round-up

No failure is final. Life is long, and you'll always have the chance to play again – as Rashford, Sancho and Saka learned when they returned to the pitch for England later in 2021. The lesson? It's not the failure that gets you – it's your reaction. And that reaction is our choice. Everyone fails, but only high performers know how to thrive through it.

Reflections:

_____

_____

_____

_____

_____

_____

_____

_____

_____

_____

_____

_____

_____

Flexibility

FLEXIBLE PERSPECTIVE

Last week's focus was **failure**. We examined how failure is inevitable, which means that the trick is knowing how to respond constructively. What did you learn?

_____

_____

_____

Think about your **goals** for the year. What have you done in the past week to help you achieve them?

_____

_____

_____

This week's focus is **flexible perspective**. We'll be examining how to think creatively and flexibly when we encounter problems. What does flexible perspective mean to you?

_____

_____

_____

_____

Do

This exercise is a puzzle. Look at the images below.

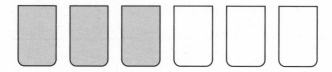

The first three glasses are full of liquid; the next three are empty. The game is to move the glasses so that the full and empty ones alternate, but there's a catch: you can only move one glass. Can you do it?

_____

_____

_____

_____

For many people, this problem seems insurmountable. Most try to move the second full glass to sit in between two empty glasses, only to realise that this still leaves two full glasses next to each other. But there's a solution: pour the liquid from the second glass into the second-to-last glass, then put the second glass back in its original place.

Did you struggle to solve this problem? That's functional fixedness. In your head, you only imagined changing the glasses' places – you weren't flexible enough to imagine pouring the liquid. This week, we will examine how high performers overcome that fixedness and think more flexibly.

Inspire

'If everybody runs in the same direction, then eventually the wheel is going to gain some momentum.'

Toto Wolff, team principal and CEO of the Mercedes-AMG Petronas F1 team

Think

High performers are problem solvers. Think of some of the greatest innovators of our time: Thomas Edison working out how to produce light without combustion, Marie Curie pioneering the study of radioactivity, the Wright brothers achieving the first powered flight. In each case, these innovators encountered a problem – a world dependent on cumbersome candles and gas lamps, a lack of understanding about how atoms fit together, the irritating fact that birds could fly but humans couldn't – and, in each case, they came up with a creative and audacious solution.

The way they solved these problems was through flexibility – coming up with new ways of approaching an old question. Reflect on the problems you have encountered recently and how you confronted them. How creative were you?

Inspire

'If you don't believe it yourself, no one else is going to believe you.'

Kasper Schmeichel, goalkeeper for Leicester City and Denmark

Do

Most of us possess a fixed model of the world in our head and we react according to that fixed model. Psychologists call these mental models 'heuristics'. Think of them as rules of thumb – simple problem-solving strategies that allow us to make sense of our surroundings. They can be useful, but they can also prevent us from being creative.

In the first column below, write something you do each day simply because 'That's what I always do.' It could be what you have for breakfast, the way you walk to work, or what you do in a five-minute break. In the column next to it, try to come up with a way to improve your approach – however small. It's the first step towards thinking flexibly about the big questions in our lives.

Today I . . .	Tomorrow I will . . .

Think

The Nobel-prize winning behavioural economist Daniel Kahneman became famous for identifying dozens of heuristics that we use to navigate the world. For example, humans consistently underestimate the amount of time it will take to finish a task. We are more influenced by potential losses than potential gains. And we tend to judge the likelihood of events based on how easily we can visualise them. Can you think of any heuristics – or 'rules of thumb' – that you use to make sense of your surroundings? In what ways are they helpful, and in what ways do they prevent you from thinking creatively?

GROWTH MINDSET

Last week's focus was **flexible perspective**. We tried to demonstrate that being flexible – and seeing through your 'heuristic biases' – is integral to becoming a high performer. What did you learn?

_____

_____

_____

Think about your **goals** for the year. What have you done in the past week to help you achieve them? What might you have done differently?

_____

_____

_____

This week's focus is **growth mindset**. The Stanford professor Carol Dweck defines a growth mindset as 'believing that your most basic abilities can be developed through dedication and hard work'. What does growth mindset mean to you?

_____

_____

_____

Do

Carol Dweck, the world-renowned professor who coined the term 'growth mindset', says that you can work out your own type of mindset using a simple test. Read the following four sentences and see which rings truest:

1. You are a certain kind of person, and there is not much that can be done to really change that.
2. You can do things differently, but the important parts of who you are can't really be changed.
3. No matter what kind of person you are, you can always change substantially.
4. You can always change basic things about the kind of person you are.

Dweck says that if you're nearer to the first statement, you have a 'fixed mindset': you assume the way things are now is how they'll always be. If you're nearer to the fourth, you have a 'growth mindset' – and you probably believe in your own ability to learn new skills. Where on the spectrum do you fall? What about some of your friends and colleagues? Mark your positions on the below line.

---

1   2   3   4

Inspire

'Your overall goal is you want that person, that organisation, that culture, to grow.'

Mel Marshall, Loughborough national lead coach for swimming

Think

Dweck argues that people with a growth mindset are more likely to achieve success – because they always dare to learn new skills. They consistently try new things, even when they know that these things might be hard at first. What three new things are you going to try this week?

_____

_____

_____

_____

_____

_____

_____

_____

_____

_____

Inspire

'Leadership is about giving people belief that you can do it. Just having someone saying, "Come on, you can do this."'

Ben Ainslie, winner of four Olympic golds and skipper of the INEOS sailing team

Do

In your journey to a growth mindset, you'll need to get used to failing – and failing often. Failure, after all, is how we learn. In the below grid, use the space on the left to identify a way you've failed in the past few months. Now, try to reframe it: on the right, identify what you learned from that supposed 'failure'. Think about it: was the failure that bad – or was it part of your journey to high performance?

The failure	The lesson

Think

When did you last find yourself thinking, 'I can't do that'? If you have a fixed mindset, probably quite recently. But the good news is that a fixed outlook isn't something you're struck with. A growth mindset is something you can learn.

Carol Dweck's brilliant TED talk offers a simple way to do so: by adding the word 'yet' to the end of your sentences. In the space below, write down three times you've recently said 'I can't do that.' Then go back over the list and write the word 'yet' at the end of each line. Now think: does the task still feel so daunting, or are these skills more easily reached than you might have thought?

YIN-YANG

Last week's focus was **growth mindset**. We looked at the difference between fixed and growth mindsets, and the relationship between these mindsets and high performance. What did you learn?

_____

_____

_____

Think about your **goals** for the year. What have you done in the past week to help you achieve them?

_____

_____

_____

This week's focus is **yin–yang**. We'll explore another way to get a flexible perspective: by drawing on the insights of people who see the world very differently from you, just like the opposite but complementary forces of 'yin' and 'yang' in Chinese philosophy. What does yin–yang mean to you?

_____

_____

_____

Inspire

'When you get tunnel vision, you keep doing things exactly the same way – and get exactly the same results. That's why we need our team – because everyone has a different way of doing things.'

Mandy Hickson, RAF fighter pilot,
life coach and author

Think

Olympic sailing champion Ben Ainslie told us on the podcast that his first foray into team leadership wasn't great: 'To start off with, if I'm brutally honest, I was rubbish at it.' But Ben turned his team around, all by bringing together the different perspectives of different parts of the team – one half American, one half British. Have you ever solved a problem by getting the opinion of someone who sees things very differently from you? What effect did their distinctive outlook have on your thinking?

Do

How can we bring an outsider's opposite perspective to every problem we encounter? This exercise offers one way – by looking through the other end of the telescope. Write down a goal or ambition that you've been struggling to realise. Around the first telescope, explain how you would usually go about getting there. Then, in the second, get creative: think of how your most wildly different acquaintance would look at the issue – perhaps with a diametrically opposing perspective. Can you come up with a different way of seeing things?

The goal: _____

Inspire

'Find people who can accept their strong and weaker points – who are happy to work in a yin–yang way with others.'

Holly Tucker, co-founder of Not On The High Street

Think

Teams that have lots of different viewpoints tend to do better than teams that have just one. Psychologists call this 'cognitive diversity'. In one article in the *Harvard Business Review*, a pair of academics analysed the performance of 100 different groups in a variety of different settings. Almost without fail, the wider the array of views in the group, the better their performance. Why? Because great minds think differently.

Think about the teams you work with. Are the more cognitively diverse teams more effective? Why?

_____

_____

_____

_____

_____

_____

_____

_____

Do

In the diagram below, write the names of people you interact with frequently in your job or team. The left–right axis is about how similar they are to you: do you see things the same way? The up–down axis is about how much you get done when you're with them: is it a productive relationship?

If the science of 'cognitive diversity' is to be believed, then you'll probably find that the people whom you work best with are the ones with whom you have less in common. But there are always exceptions: What does your diagram say about your working style?

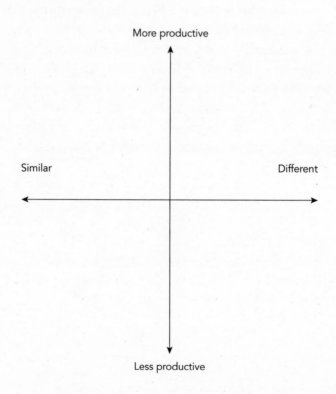

MAD SCIENTIST THINKING

Last week's focus was **yin–yang**. We argued that great minds think differently – and so the best way to break out of your fixed mindset is to work with people who see the world in ways that are alien to yours. What did you learn?

_____

_____

_____

Think about your **goals** for the year. What have you done in the past week to help you achieve them?

_____

_____

_____

This week's focus is **mad scientist thinking**. This is a final way we can break out of our heuristic traps: by forcing ourselves to look at things in an eccentric, off-the-wall way. What does mad scientist thinking mean to you?

_____

_____

_____

Think

It's human nature to get trapped in a particular way of doing things, and lose sight of alternative, more creative solutions. We become wedded to one way of resolving an issue, and then can't imagine any alternatives. Can you think of a problem you have never been able to solve? What do you think is stopping you?

_____

_____

_____

_____

_____

_____

_____

_____

_____

Inspire

'We have balance – an ability to appreciate both sides of the coin.'

Holly Tucker, co-founder of Not On The High Street

Do

Write a problem you need to solve or an issue that's on your mind in the central circle. It could be related to how to get on at work, how to share a difficult piece of news or a big personal issue. Around the circle, write as many possible solutions as you can think of – at least six.

These 'solutions' do not have to be tangible, rational or even achievable: grab your boss by the lapels and demand a promotion, write your message on the sky in jet-fumes – anything. The point is to encourage your inner mad scientist to come up with as many ideas as possible, however crazy. As you do so, something a bit more practical might come to mind too.

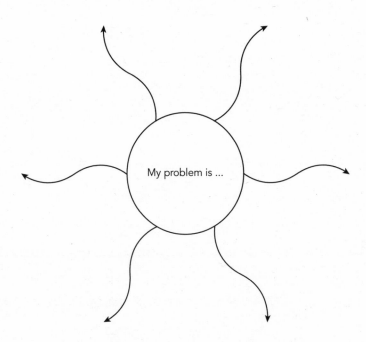

My problem is ...

Think

When Premier League goalkeeper Kasper Schmeichel felt his career had stagnated, he 'restarted' his professional life by taking a new job – three divisions down the league. His reset paid dividends and he became one of the most respected keepers in the country with Premier League- and FA Cup-winning Leicester City. 'I didn't prove anyone wrong. I proved myself right,' he told us.

There's a lesson here for everyone. Schmeichel's professional restart hints at how we can all use creativity to get out of a rut. What would a reset look like in your life?

_____

_____

_____

_____

_____

_____

_____

_____

_____

_____

_____

_____

_____

_____

Do

Marcelino Sambé, principal male dancer of the Royal Ballet, suffered an injury that prevented him dancing for months on end. But it didn't get in his way – because Sambé reframed the injury as an opportunity to grow in other areas of his life.

We can all reframe our problems as chances to get a new perspective – we just need the right approach. Write down a setback you've experienced in your own life – a problem at work, perhaps. Next, reflect on a positive way in which your behaviour changed as a result. Can you reframe your problem as an opportunity?

My setback was: _____

_____

_____

_____

My behaviour changed by: _____

_____

_____

_____

Inspire

'The most dangerous phrase in the language of a high performer is "We've always done it this way." '

Toto Wolff, team principal and CEO of the Mercedes-AMG Petronas F1 team

LESSON IN REVIEW
FLEXIBILITY

Last week's focus was **mad scientist thinking**. We explored how to break out of the heuristic traps that define our lives by thinking about things in an off-the-wall way. What did you learn?

_____

_____

_____

Think about your **goals** for the year. What have you done in the past week to help you achieve them?

_____

_____

_____

This week we're going to summarise what we've learnt about **flexibility**. Has this lesson made you see flexibility differently?

_____

_____

_____

Do

If you find yourself getting stuck, the worst response is to go with the crowd. Great minds rarely think alike. The best way to break through your heuristic traps is to see things from a new perspective.

Here is a round table. In the centre, write down a question you've been grappling with over the past few months. Use the spaces around the table to write down how the eight most different people you can think of would advise you to solve it – the more varied the answers the better. Now take a step back and think: which of these methods feels most creative? Might that just be the solution you're looking for?

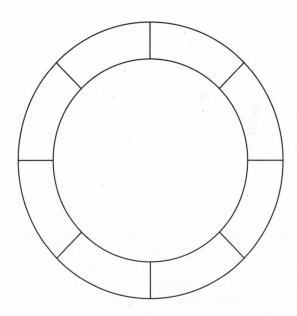

Think

When the legendary Mercedes boss Toto Wolff first arrived at the F1 team's HQ, he was greeted by old newspapers and dirty coffee cups. Focusing on the small, often-unnoticed details – like keeping the room tidy – fed into a giant transformation: winning seven consecutive double world championships.

By focusing on the things that everyone else ignores, you can make a big difference. What small things in your life could you change?

_____

_____

_____

_____

_____

_____

_____

_____

Inspire

'Sometimes seeing something just a little bit differently and from a different angle can give you that "aha" moment.'

Mary-Christine Sungaila, human rights lawyer

Think

Think of the most flexible person you know. Do they draw upon the methods we've introduced in this chapter – from building a growth mindset to embracing yin–yang thinking? If not, what does make them so creative?

_____

_____

_____

_____

_____

_____

_____

_____

_____

_____

_____

_____

_____

_____

_____

Inspire

'When you're in tough situations, the last thing you should do is do what everybody else is doing.'

Steve Morgan, businessman and philanthropist

Lesson round-up

When we encounter problems, we often use tried-and-tested shortcuts to solve them. These heuristics can be useful, but can also prevent us from being creative. Effective problem-solving is all about smashing through your heuristics and gaining a flexible perspective.

How can we learn to think flexibly?

1. Growth mindset: convince yourself that the puzzles you encounter *can* be solved. It's not that you can't do it – it's that you can't do it *yet*.
2. Yin–yang: ask the opinion of someone completely unlike you. Do they have a different take?
3. Mad-scientist thinking: if you were encountering this problem without any preconceptions, what would you do?

Above all, remember that seeing things in an unusual way isn't the problem – it's the solution. High performers do things differently.

RECOVERY

In 1959, the American DJ Peter Tripp sat in his radio booth for 201 straight hours without sleeping to raise money for a children's charity. The other beneficiaries of Tripp's remarkable feat were sleep scientists, who were intrigued by how his body would cope with the ordeal. A group of researchers closely monitored Tripp's reactions, including his brainwave patterns. By the end of his 'wake-a-thon', he was taking drugs to keep himself awake and suffering from hallucinations. Scientists said that his brain was in the state it would normally be in during a deep sleep cycle – except Tripp was wide awake.

In the weeks and months that followed, Tripp's behaviour started to transform. Soon afterwards he lost his job. A few months later he divorced. Friends described him as a changed man – with the changes starting during those 201 long hours.

You don't have to undergo a wake-a-thon to realise that giving yourself time to recover is crucial. Sports scientists are clear: recovery is critical to optimum performance. And it's not just sleep. As the former US soccer player and two-time Olympic gold winner Carli Lloyd put it, 'Recovery is around the clock. Are you sleeping enough? Are you hydrating enough? Are you stretching? Are you eating well?' She built recovery into her routine – and credits it as a key factor in her success.

This week, we're going to explore the science of recovery. According to Kris Swartzendruber of Michigan State University, effective recovery has three components – short term (hours), long term (days or weeks) and sleep – and we'll be offering insights into each. We'll show that high performance isn't just about exerting yourself. It's about giving yourself the space to heal.

Reflections:

_____

_____

_____

_____

_____

_____

_____

_____

_____

_____

_____

_____

_____

_____

_____

_____

_____

_____

_____

Think

Have you ever pushed yourself too far? Perhaps you over-exerted yourself at work, or gave yourself an injury on the sports field. Use the space below to reflect on what happened, and what you learned. Would things have gone better if you had taken the time recover?

_____

_____

_____

_____

_____

_____

_____

_____

_____

_____

Inspire

'It's great to have that mentality to push hard. But for me, the trick was learning when to push and when to rest.'

Chris Hoy, six-time Olympic gold-winning cyclist

Do

This diagram will help you to integrate rest, recovery and sleep into your daily routine. Inside the arrows, write what you will do to make sure you are prioritising each area of your life equally. For example, if you want to make the most of your work, you might write 'Log out of social media while working'; for rest, you could say 'Avoid coffee during down-time' and for sleep, you could write 'Go to bed before 11pm.' What will you do?

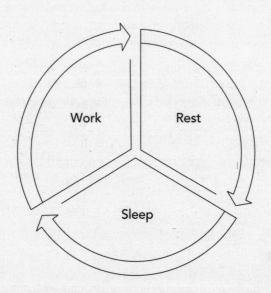

Inspire

'The solution to over-training was understanding everything outside of exercise too. What are you doing the other twenty hours of the day?'

Will Ahmed, founder and CEO of Whoop

Do

Marathon runners often talk about 'hitting the wall', when they feel like they simply can't go on any more. In 2016, Alistair Brownlee famously helped his brother Jonny over the line at the World Triathlon Series in Mexico. Jonny had hit the wall and could hardly stand, let alone run. But you need not be a professional athlete to understand the power of the wall. In the below diagram, write down any signs that you might be pushing yourself too far. Learn to spot them – and do something about them before it's too late.

Lesson round-up

Remember the three components of recovery: short term, long term and sleep. High performers know that each one needs to be given the attention it deserves. That means paying attention to your days off, your social life and even your sleep. All too often, we equate high performance with overexertion. The truth is that high performance is as much about rest as about work.

Reflections:

_____

_____

_____

_____

_____

_____

_____

_____

_____

_____

_____

_____

_____

Consistency

TRADEMARK BEHAVIOURS

Last week's focus was **recovery**. We discussed the importance of the three stages of recovery: short term, long term and sleep. What did you learn?

_____

_____

_____

Think about your **goals** for the year. What have you done in the past week to help you achieve them?

_____

_____

_____

This week's focus is **trademark behaviours**. We'll demonstrate that high performers always have a few non-negotiable features of their approach – features that we call 'trademark behaviours'. What does this concept mean to you?

_____

_____

_____

_____

Inspire

'Consistent habits like timekeeping set standards of behaviour. Slipping standards have an insidious impact on performance.'

Clive Woodward, former rugby international and World Cup-winning head coach

Think

So many of our high performers homed in on the importance of timekeeping. If you want to master high performance, they told us, discipline with your time is everything. Think about your own approach to timekeeping. Are you always on time? Early? Late? What does that say about you?

Do

A trademark behaviour is one that you commit to unequivocally. When a situation gets tough and everything else disintegrates, the trademark behaviours remain in place. Your commitment to these behaviours, through thick and thin, makes for high performance.

What are your non-negotiables? List them below. Always remember: make them simple, make them clear and make them count.

Non-negotiable 1: _____

Non-negotiable 2: _____

Non-negotiable 3: _____

Think

The legendary Scottish rugby player and coach Ian McGeechan offers a simple way to think about consistency: 'world-class basics'. These are the simple behaviours that he claims underpin all high performance. Within a team, they involve playing to your strengths: 'Delivering something that you know you can do or needs to be done to actually make a difference.' Apply this concept to your own life. What are the basics that underpin all your successes within the teams you're part of?

_____

_____

_____

Inspire

'The only way to win is through consistency. Consistent messages, consistent behaviours and consistent consequences.'

Shaun Wane, former rugby league player, and head coach of England's national team

Do

Clive Woodward had a very strict half-time routine for his rugby team – it was one of his non-negotiables. You can use Woodward's 'second-half thinking' method in your own life. Think of the natural five-minutes breaks that come in your day – when you get up from your desk to get a coffee, for example. Is there a way to use this time constructively by developing a similar ritual? What will you do with this time, every time?

0–1 minutes
Behaviour: _____

2–3 minutes
Behaviour: _____

4–5 minutes
Behaviour: _____

THE POWER OF HABIT

Last week's focus was **trademark behaviours**. We took an important step by listing our non-negotiables and explored why they matter. What did you learn?

_____

_____

_____

Think about your **goals** for the year. What have you done in the past week to help you achieve them?

_____

_____

_____

This week's focus is **the power of habit**. We'll explore where our habits come from, and what effect they have on our lives. What does the power of habit mean to you?

_____

_____

_____

_____

Inspire

'I've got an opportunity every day to get the best out of the day.'

Adam Peaty, Olympic champion swimmer and world record holder

Think

Habits are everywhere. They are the force that allow us to turn our trademark behaviours from lofty ideals into deep-rooted features of our life. Use the space below to reflect on people you know and the habits you associate with them – good and bad. Where do you think these habits come from?

_____

_____

_____

_____

_____

_____

_____

_____

_____

_____

_____

Do

The science of habits is surprisingly simple. As Charles Duhigg shows in his seminal bestseller *The Power of Habit*, they're a loop made up of cue, routine and reward. Take having a cup of tea and a biscuit at 2pm: there's a cue (you spot that it's 2pm, you're feeling peckish), you unthinkingly wander into the kitchen (routine) and you get the delicious taste of warm tea and sugary treat (reward). The whole thing is a never-ending loop: because of that tasty reward, you're more likely to experience the cue in future – and so the cycle continues.

Once you start looking, you'll find that these cycles are everywhere. In the grid below, succinctly write down the cue, routine and reward for some of your daily habits.

Cue	Routine	Reward
Habit 1:		
Habit 2:		
Habit 3:		

Inspire

'You want to perform well? Then commit.'

Steven Gerrard, Aston Villa manager and former Liverpool and England footballer

Think

Never fear: the bad-habit cycle isn't inevitable. Once you understand the science of habits, it becomes easier to build good behaviours and eradicate bad ones.

Identifying the cues for your bad behaviour is the first step. When Tracy Neville became manager of the England Roses netball team, she issued an edict: the dressing room mattered. She changed one cue in her players' day: before you leave the dressing room, tidy up your locker. This led to dozens of other positive behavioural cues through the day.

Have you ever found that a simple 'cue' like this transformed your behaviour? What effect did it have on your life?

_____

_____

_____

_____

_____

_____

_____

Do

We can use a simple prompt to set ourselves on a chosen behaviour path. The psychologists Peter Gollwitzer and Veronika Brandstätter once hacked people's abilities to meet a goal by using an 'action trigger' – that is, a commitment to do something at a set time. In practice, that means using the simple formula, 'After I do X, I will then do Y' – for example, 'After I get up, I will then eat fruit for breakfast.' By settling on the right action triggers, you can build new behaviours into the fabric of your day.

Use the space below to write down three formulas for you to follow tomorrow. Ideally, make them consecutive, so the action of the first sets you on a course for more.

*After I get up, I will*_____

*After I*_____

*I will*_____

*After I*_____

*I will*_____

HIGH-PERFORMANCE IDENTITY

Last week's focus was **the power of habit**. We looked at the habit cycle, and how to hack its cue stage to build better ones. What did you learn?

_____

_____

_____

Think about your **goals** for the year. What have you done in the past week to help you achieve them?

_____

_____

_____

This week's focus is **high-performance identity**. As we'll discover, the best way to build good habits is to integrate high performance into your identity. High performance should become an integral part of your sense of self. What does a high-performance identity mean to you?

_____

_____

_____

Do

Use the circles below to write down the words that underpin your sense of self. That could be how you see yourself (teammate, mum, business partner), or how the people in your life see you (wife, golfer, shoulder to cry on). Next, circle the two that you think are most important. Is that who you want to be? Does this feel like a high-performance identity?

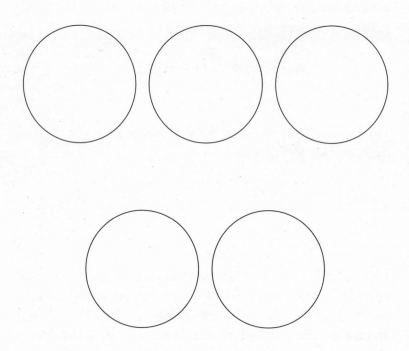

Think

Rio Ferdinand undertook an identity change after seeking help from his new boss at Leeds United, David O'Leary. He chose to focus on building an *identity* as a world-beating athlete, integrating high performance into his deepest sense of who he is.

If we're serious about building consistent behaviours in the long term, we need nothing less than to change our sense of who we are. Think about people you admire. How do they view themselves? What can you learn from how they've made high performance part of who they are?

_____

_____

_____

_____

_____

_____

_____

_____

Inspire

'In a weird way, life is about teaching you that you don't know much. You've got to know what you don't know.'

Lee Child, international bestselling author

Think

The Stanford professor James March undertook research into why people make decisions, particularly ones that do not directly benefit them. He identified that although some decisions are made based on the outcome (a cold, reasoned, analytical approach), most decisions were made based on identity. In other words, we make decisions by asking ourselves: 'What would someone like me do in this situation?' What do you think is the identity that underpins your decisions?

_____

_____

_____

_____

_____

_____

_____

_____

Inspire

'You become what you think about.'

Aldo Kane, world-record-setting adventurer and former Royal Marines Commando

Do

Write some choices you have made recently in the left-hand column, from the small (second helping of dinner?) to the life-changing (apply for a new job?). Then in the right-hand column reflect on whether you think it was a 'consequence' decision (i.e. focused on the outcome) or an 'identity' decision (which you made because of your sense of self). Now think about those decisions again. Would you make the same choices again?

Action	Decision

EVERY WAKING MOMENT

Last week's focus was **high-performance identity**. We looked at how our sense of self drives the choices we make, which means that we need to come to identify as high performers. What did you learn?

_____

_____

_____

Think about your **goals** for the year. What have you done in the past week to help you achieve them?

_____

_____

_____

This week's focus is **every waking moment**. As Damian is fond of saying, 'What is done in the shadows reveals itself in the light': if you commit to a behaviour during your down-time, then it will come naturally when it matters most. What does this concept mean to you?

_____

_____

_____

Inspire

'Having an identity is so important for anybody: knowing where they're going to go, what they're going to do.'

Kelly Holmes, Olympic and Commonwealth
running champion

Think

Kelly Jones, frontman of Stereophonics, told us that his identity as a musician came to him early: 'My earliest memories are of making up little melodies that I knew weren't anybody else's.' Even at a very young age, his every waking moment was given over to music. Think back through your childhood: are there any events that indicated you had a vocation too?

_____

_____

_____

_____

_____

_____

_____

_____

_____

Do

If you're serious about building a behaviour in the long term, try not to frame it as a one-off choice. Instead, frame it as a series of questions about the type of person you want to be. A good way to tackle a problem situation is to use the following prompts:

- Who am I?
- What kind of situation is this?
- What would someone like me do in this situation?

Think of a trying time you expect to find yourself in soon, and use the prompts to guide your response. Remember, what is done in the shadows reveals itself in the light: if you commit to *being* a certain type of person, you'll always exhibit the behaviours of that person.

Situation: _____

_____

Who am I? _____

_____

What kind of situation is this? _____

_____

What would someone like me do in this situation? _____

_____

_____

Inspire

'The moment you start holding back and neglect your training, you will feel unprepared. I don't ever let myself feel that way.'

Marcelino Sambé, principal male dancer of the
Royal Ballet

Do

It's not enough to commit to your trademark behaviours part-time – you need to work on them every day. If you have rehearsed your trademark behaviours in every waking moment – at work and at home, with colleagues and with family – you'll have learnt to exhibit them unthinkingly, even when you're under unimaginable pressure.

Here, reflect on how you are you going to practise your trademarks in moments of calm – so that they come easily in moments of stress. What will you do to build your trademarks into your life?

Behaviour 1: _____

Practice: _____

Behaviour 2: _____

Practice: _____

Behaviour 3: _____

Practice: _____

Think

The route to consistent behaviour is commitment. Have you ever given yourself over to a behaviour in every waking moment of your life? Did it become easier to exhibit the behaviour the more you committed to it?

_____

_____

_____

_____

_____

_____

_____

_____

_____

_____

_____

_____

_____

_____

_____

_____

LESSON IN REVIEW
CONSISTENCY

Last week's focus was **every waking moment**. We explored why it isn't enough to commit to your trademark behaviours sometimes – you have to commit to them all the time. What did you learn?

_____

_____

_____

Think about your **goals** for the year. What have you done in the past week to help you achieve them?

_____

_____

_____

This week we're going to summarise what we've learnt about **consistency**. Has this lesson made you see it differently?

_____

_____

_____

_____

Inspire

'Doing the right thing – every single minute of every single day.'

Phil Neville, head coach of Inter Miami and former Manchester United, Everton and England footballer

Think

High performers understand the power of commitment. On the podcast, people from ballet dancers to entrepreneurs have told us about their trademark behaviours: how they found them, how they committed to them and how they built them into their identities.

You can do the same. How will you make sure you commit to your trademarks every day of the year?

_____

_____

_____

_____

_____

_____

_____

_____

_____

Do

Earlier we explored the power of the 'habit loop', which divides all consistent behaviours into a cycle of cue, response and reward. Around the edges of the diagram below, write down how your trademark behaviours have changed since we explored the habit cycle. Have you managed to introduce new cues? Has it rippled through to your behaviour?

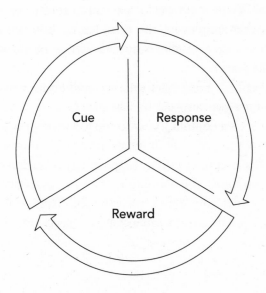

Inspire

'Courage. It's not about running in front of a bus to save a pram. It's the courage to do the small things and to do them well, to the best of your ability, every single day.'

Aldo Kane, former sniper commando, adventurer and TV presenter

Do

One question about consistency remains: what happens if you do slip up? Many high performers are mindful of this issue too. Sure, they emphasise the need for consistency, but they acknowledge that everyone is human. Everyone lapses in their trademarks sometimes.

But never fear. High performance isn't about never failing. It's about how you respond to that first failure. A slip-up isn't a full stop – it's a comma. Next to the top prompt below, write down an area of your life in which you've been known to slip up – whether it's punctuality, skipping a gym session or having a dessert you know you shouldn't. Underneath, reflect on how you'll make sure you don't repeat the slip. And remember the lesson from habits expert James Clear: 'Never miss twice.'

Slip-up: _____

_____

Response: _____

_____

Lesson round-up

High performers are consistent. They have a handful of non-negotiable trademark behaviours – and they stick to them. But how can all of us build trademark behaviours into our lives?

1. To make your trademarks effective, turn them into habits by building behavioural cues (or 'action triggers') into your environment.
2. To make your trademarks sustainable, incorporate them into your identity. Imagine an ideal version of yourself, then ask: what would they do in this situation?
3. To make your trademarks long-lasting, commit to them every waking moment. Remember Damian's maxim: what is done in the shadows reveals itself in the light.

Above all, remember this simple motto: never miss twice. Yes, on some days your habits might slip. But if high performers miss one day, they never miss a second.

DIET

According to the *New Scientist*, 'Our diets are more homogenous than at any other point in human history.' Over the past 150 years, what we eat has changed more dramatically than at any point in the last million years of evolution. Gone are the days when we would eat a wide array of fruit, meat and grain, sourced locally from the land. Instead, we consume an ever-narrowing number of ultra-processed factory foods, much of it flown in from around the world. The effects on our health – let alone the planet – are corrosive.

All the science says that a diverse, balanced and constantly changing diet is integral to human health. When we interviewed gastroenterologist and *MasterChef* winner Saliha Mahmood-Ahmed, she was unambiguous. 'The science tells us that a good, varied diet involves a diverse array of different compounds, different chemicals, different plant-based products,' she said. 'We're not talking about even having five fruit or veggies a day – we're talking about really going for it: packing five fruit and veg into one meal a day, and really increasing the diversity of what we eat.'

The trouble is that, even though ever greater numbers of us are worried about our diets, we are also easily distracted by the non-stop influx of health fads: cutting out meat or dairy, obsessively counting calories, making sure we eat X amount of carbs and Y amount of protein. Sure, many of these approaches may have their benefits, but they're only ever going to be a short-term solution to a long-term problem. A healthy approach to food is all about building a diverse, sustainable diet in the long term.

So, this 'In Focus' session isn't going to advocate any one 'hack' to your diet. Nor is it going to tell you precisely what to eat. Instead, we're going to invite you to reflect on what you eat now and offer some gentle tips on where to go next. A high-performance approach to diet isn't about 'dieting', per se. It's about subtly recalibrating how you think about food.

Reflections:

_____

_____

_____

_____

_____

_____

_____

_____

_____

_____

_____

_____

_____

_____

_____

Think

Think about a time in your life when you felt particularly healthy. Can you recall what your diet was like at that time? How did it differ from what you eat now?

Do

This exercise will help you to recalibrate your diet away from factory foods and towards more natural and diverse sources of nutrition. Many of the nutrition experts on our podcast recommend maximising your intake of unprocessed food and staying away from ultra-processed products whenever possible. Write down how many of each of the food types you have eaten in the past twenty-four hours. Do you think you're getting the balance right?

Ultra-processed	Processed	Unprocessed
E.g. pre-packaged meals, breakfast cereals with added sugar, confectionery, biscuits, buns, flavoured yogurt	E.g. smoked and cured meats, cheese, fresh bread, salted or sugared nuts, tinned fruit, beer, wine	E.g. fruit, vegetables, nuts, seeds, grains, beans, natural animal products (eggs, fish, milk, meat), plain yogurt, cornflakes, shredded wheat

Inspire

'At the end of the day, we eat food, not numbers.'

Rhiannon Lambert, nutritionist and bestselling author

Think

Where our food comes from matters. Constantly nipping round the corner to the local chippie will lead to a less diverse diet than growing your own fruit or getting fresh veg from a local source. Where do you source your food? If you wanted to build a more diverse diet, where would you go instead?

_____

_____

_____

_____

_____

_____

_____

_____

_____

_____

_____

_____

_____

Do

Nutritional diversity is important for your health. In the pie chart (no pun intended), write examples of each type of food that you have eaten this week – and assess whether your diet is as wide-ranging as it might be. You may want to come back to this chart in the coming weeks and months, to see if you're heading in the right direction.

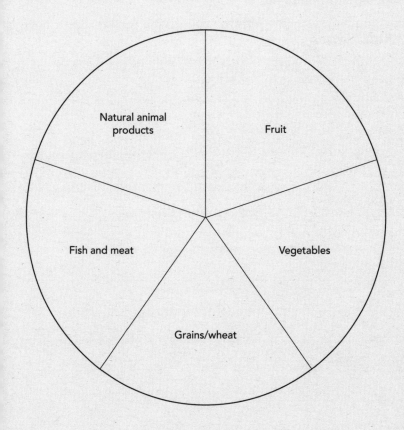

Lesson round-up

The goal this week has been to focus on a diverse, sustainable diet. We've given you no recipes or shopping lists – just a few simple tips that might help you improve what you eat. The trick is to remember that diet matters everywhere: from the health of your gut to the speed of your brain, from your mood in the morning to your energy levels in the evening. By building a high-performance diet, you can help yourself to build a high-performance life.

Reflections:

_____

_____

_____

_____

_____

_____

_____

_____

_____

_____

_____

_____

Leadership

THE POWER OF TEAMS

Last week's focus was **diet**. We looked at how all of us can build a more diverse diet – and why that matters. What did you learn?

_____

_____

_____

Think about your **goals** for the year. What have you done in the past week to help you achieve them?

_____

_____

_____

This week's focus is **the power of teams**. So far in this book, we've discussed how to become a high-achieving individual. But none of us succeeds or fails by ourselves – we do so as part of a group. What does the power of teams mean to you?

_____

_____

_____

Inspire

'Most people complain and complain and complain. Opportunity presents itself, and they're not ready.'

Siya Kolisi, captain of South Africa's 2019 Rugby World Cup-winning team

Think

Siya Kolisi's early life was defined by great hardship, as he spent his youth in the townships of Port Elizabeth, South Africa. But he went on to become the first Black man to captain the South African rugby team, and did so extremely successfully. He told us on the podcast that he took enormous pride and energy from being part of the Springboks. Think about any teams you are part of either professionally or personally. How do they make you feel?

Do

In the left-hand column, write the names of the most high-performing teams you know. They can be teams you have worked in, ones you've seen first-hand – even great teams from history. In the right-hand column write what you think made them excel. Can you spot a recipe for great teamwork?

Team	Characteristics

Inspire

'I know I'm not the smartest guy in the room – and I don't have to be. I just have to surround myself with like-minded people.'

Dilbagh Gill, CEO and team principal of
Mahindra Racing

Think

According to Reid Hoffman, the co-founder of LinkedIn, 'No matter how brilliant your mind or strategy, if you're playing a solo game, you'll always lose out to a team.' He was right: teams can make or break any high performer. Use this space to think about the people you work with. How well do you gel together?

_____

_____

_____

_____

_____

_____

_____

_____

Do

In each bubble, write a team you have been part of – at work, with family or friends, sports teams. Alongside each team name, draw an arrow, pointing upwards if you thought the team was effective, downwards if it wasn't, and sideways if you aren't sure. When you've finished, take a second to think about the type of team that seemed to elicit your best work. Do all the up arrows have anything in common?

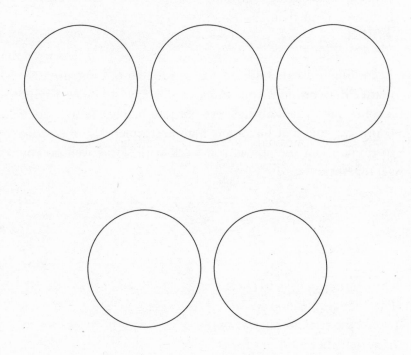

BHAGS

Last week's focus was the **power of teams**. We argued that teams are the engine that allow high performing individuals to turbo-charge their success. What did you learn?

_____

_____

_____

Think about your **goals** for the year. What have you done in the past week to help you achieve them?

_____

_____

_____

This week's focus is **BHAGs** – or 'big, hairy, audacious goals'. The management academics Jim Collins and Jerry Porras coined the term to refer to the biggest, most ambitious objectives that they said mark out a brilliant organisation. What does this concept mean to you?

_____

_____

_____

Think

Collins and Porras defined a BHAG as 'an audacious ten-to-thirty-year goal to progress towards an envisioned future'. Their research showed that massive, motivating objectives distinguish good companies from great ones. Does your place of work have a clear focus? If not, why not?

_____

_____

_____

_____

_____

_____

_____

Do

A leader's job isn't to control every facet of a team's behaviour. It is to identify a BHAG and pinpoint the handful of behaviours that will get the team there. What BHAGs would you like your team to adopt?

*BHAG 1:*_____

*BHAG 2:*_____

*BHAG 3:*_____

Inspire

'The negotiables are wide and varied. There's way less non-negotiables – certain things are important.'

Sean Dyche, former Premier League manager

Think

American psychologists Chip and Dan Heath say that a BHAG's power lies in its size: the goal is so massive that it can't help but inspire. Have you ever worked in a group that had no BHAG? What effect do you think it had?

_____

_____

_____

_____

_____

_____

_____

_____

_____

_____

Inspire

'The individual and the collective go hand in hand.'

Rob Baxter, director of rugby for Exeter Chiefs and former player

Do

The commander's intent is a clear, straightforward statement that is included in every written order given in the US Army. It specifies the goal of an operation. Although it rarely specifies the precise actions a team should take, it describes the behaviours that soldiers might be required to exhibit.

Fill in the declaration of intent below using an example from your life.

Declaration of intent

The objective is to:

_____

_____

_____

To achieve it, I am going to:

_____

_____

_____

NO-BULLSHIT LEADERSHIP

Last week's focus was **BHAGs**. We worked on identifying a giant goal for your team and thought about what it feels like to work with others. What did you learn?

_____

_____

_____

Think about your **goals** for the year. What have you done in the past week to help you achieve them?

_____

_____

_____

This week's focus is **no-bullshit leadership**. Being a leader isn't just about encouraging good behaviours; it's also about discouraging bad ones. What does no-bullshit leadership mean to you?

_____

_____

_____

_____

Inspire

'Saying "no" is a critical skill. It allows complete focus on the most important stuff.'

Tom Daley, World and Olympic diving champion,
LGBT+ activist

Think

Gymshark founder Ben Francis stepped down as CEO of the company he founded to focus on the things he loved doing. He knew his strengths – and those of his team – and adjusted everyone's roles accordingly. Think about your team. Is everyone doing what they're best at? If not, what behaviours could some members of your team cut out?

_____

_____

_____

_____

_____

_____

_____

_____

_____

Do

When the management academic Jim Collins was a graduate student, a professor asked him to conduct a simple exercise. The professor told him to imagine getting two phone calls. In the first, you learn that you have inherited $20 million, no strings attached. In the second, you learn you have a rare, incurable disease and have only ten years to live. In each case, what would you stop doing?

The professor's point was simple: the best way to live life is by cutting out the bullshit. What pointless tasks would you cut out if this happened to you? Do your answers offer a clearer sense of what really matters?

First, I would stop: _____

Second, I would stop: _____

Third, I would stop: _____

Inspire

'You need to set your ego aside and ensure the business is always put first.'

Ben Francis, entrepreneur and founder of Gymshark

Think

From social media to binge eating, many of the things we do without thinking do not help us to achieve our goals. What do you find most distracts you from achieving your objectives? What about your teammates?

_____

_____

_____

_____

_____

Do

Write down a list of the tasks you've completed at work in the past week, focusing on the ones that take more than an hour. Next, go through that list and give it a mark out of ten for how much it aligns with your goals – or, even better, your BHAG.

Divide the tasks into three categories based on the score assigned to them:

- Scores of 1–3: if a task isn't adding anything to your objectives, ask yourself whether you can stop doing it.
- Scores of 4–7: if a task is inescapable but clearly isn't helping with your objectives, try to work out if there's a way to systematically remove it from your to-do list – perhaps by delegating it.
- Scores of 8–10: if a task is in this top tier, focus on it. It should make up the bulk of your working hours.

Of course, there will be exceptions to this approach: there are some tasks that are both enragingly pointless and unavoidable. But this is a useful starting point when it comes to turning your to-do list into a to-don't list.

Task	Score (out of 10)

YOUR LIEUTENANTS

Last week's focus was **no-bullshit leadership**. We worked on cutting out tasks that don't help us to achieve our long-term goals. What did you learn?

Think about your **goals** for the year. What have you done in the past week to help you achieve them?

This week's focus is **your lieutenants**. Leadership should never be solitary; it requires finding your deputies and learning to trust them. What does finding your lieutenants mean to you?

Think

The psychologist Solomon Asch was intrigued by how we are swayed by the actions of our peers. His most fascinating insight relates to the influence of a 'supporting power'. He showed that when we're in groups, we almost invariably follow the crowd. However, if only one person breaks the mould then other members of the group will feel empowered to follow suit. Have you ever spoken out and found that more people agree with you than you'd expected? What do you think the experience says about how groups think?

_____

_____

_____

_____

_____

_____

_____

_____

Inspire

'He didn't speak so much. He led by example.'

Phil Neville, head coach of Inter Miami and former Manchester United, Everton and England footballer

Do

Cultural architect was the term the Norwegian sports psychologist Willi Railo used to refer to individuals with the power to sway the behaviour of a whole team. They are the people who set an example for the rest of the group – and so are able to change the mindset of others.

In the space below, list four of the people in a team of which you're a member. Are any of them cultural architects? Place a tick or an X next to each person. What do the cultural architects have in common?

_____ ☐

_____ ☐

_____ ☐

_____ ☐

Inspire

'A cultural architect is someone you look up to.'

_Ole Gunnar Solskjaer, former Manchester United
player and manager_

Think

Not all cultural architects operate in the same way. Some tell, others simply do. Think of the most impressive individuals you have worked with and their differing styles. Which approach was the most effective?

_____

_____

_____

_____

_____

_____

_____

_____

_____

_____

_____

_____

_____

_____

_____

_____

_____

Do

Cultural architects are marked out by three characteristics:

1. Status: instead of telling people what to do, they have an influence through their actions – because people look up to them.
2. Attitude: they will protect, even nurture, other members of the team.
3. Talent: they are the individuals who get their teammates' attention – and respect – through their sheer skill.

In the diagram below, write the names of the cultural architects you admire. What combination of status, attitude and talent do they have? Does anyone you know possess all three?

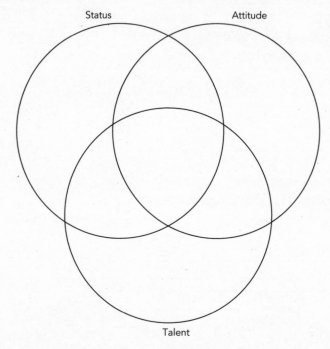

Status

Attitude

Talent

LESSON IN REVIEW
LEADERSHIP

Last week's focus was **your lieutenants.** We learned that no leader should lead alone – instead, they should find a group of 'cultural architects' to deputise for them. What did you learn?

_____

_____

_____

Think about your **goals** for the year. What have you done in the past week to help you achieve them?

_____

_____

_____

This week we're going to summarise what we've learnt about **leadership.** Has this lesson made you see it differently?

_____

_____

_____

_____

Inspire

'Actions speak louder than words.'

Kevin Sinfield, former Leeds Rhinos player and one of the most awarded captains in rugby league history

Do

Leadership takes inner strength. In your high-performance journey, there will be moments when you feel the pressure is too much. You'll be called upon to lead, and it will feel solitary – even lonely. In such moments, recall these principles of leadership and take heart. Leading isn't about obsessively controlling everything. It's about setting direction – and trusting those around you to do the right thing.

What direction do you want your team to go in? Inside the arrows below, write the behaviours that you think will help you get there.

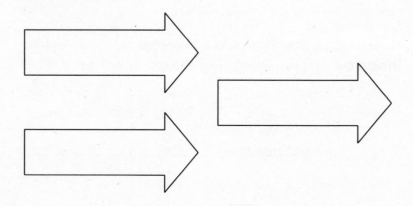

Think

One crucial element of leadership isn't about directing at all – it's about standing up for your teammates when they come under fire. Have you ever stood up for someone who has been picked on unfairly? What effect did your actions have on that individual, and the mood of the wider team?

_____

_____

_____

_____

_____

_____

_____

_____

_____

_____

Inspire

'The amount of effort and time that's gone into building the car is incredible. I'm just the final piece of that jigsaw.'

Lando Norris, F1 driver for McLaren

Lesson round-up

Leaders aren't autocrats. They set the direction and trust their teams to find the path themselves. What does this entail?

1. Leaders outline the group's objectives. Find your BHAG – big, hairy, audacious goal – and make it central to everything you do.
2. Leaders cut out the bullshit. A crucial part of leadership is directing people what *not* to do.
3. Leaders never act alone. Seek out your cultural architects – the high-status, likeable, talented individuals admired by everyone in the group – and trust them.

Remember that leadership is high-pressure, but it need never be solitary. Leaders are part of the team, not above it – and that makes leadership less scary than you might think.

EXERCISE

When John McAvoy was sent to prison for armed robbery, his future looked bleak. His life until then had been defined by crime – a vicious cycle that he seemed to have no way of breaking. Until, that was, he discovered fitness. From the confines of his prison cell, McAvoy had an epiphany. 'I started doing the cell circuits,' he told us. 'It made me feel alive.'

According to a study from the *British Journal of Pharmacology*, the benefits of physical fitness are enormous. There is 'irrefutable evidence showing the beneficial effects of exercise both to prevent and to treat several diseases,' the authors write – a phenomenon that humans have understood since at least 2,500BC. But John McAvoy didn't need an academic journal to tell him that: he was experiencing the benefits first-hand. Initially he witnessed subtle changes to his mood, then to his body, and then to his life.

Today, McAvoy is one of the leading Ironman triathletes of our time. It was a long journey. The progress was 'so tiny, so small, that sometimes you don't even notice you're getting better,' he told us. That's the approach this chapter will adopt. You won't find any ab-crunching sit-up routines, or instructions to do a set number of burpees every day. Instead, we're going to focus on the little changes we can all make to enhance our fitness, starting now.

We'll first record where you are currently, then work out the areas of your exercise routine that will be easiest to change, and finally build up to a more ambitious long-term exercise goal. Your overall objective could be big or small, but it will start with something tiny: the first step. For McAvoy, that step was in a prison cell. Yours could be anywhere: even where you're sat right now. It is never too soon to harness the power of exercise.

Reflections:

_____

_____

_____

_____

_____

_____

_____

_____

_____

_____

_____

_____

_____

_____

_____

_____

_____

_____

Think

Do you have a fitness goal? It could be anything, from running a marathon to walking three times round the local park. Write it down here – and come back to it whenever you're feeling demotivated.

_____

_____

_____

_____

_____

_____

_____

_____

Inspire

'My life revolves around my training, my nutrition, my rest – to be the best that I can be and to give myself the best chance of being the best.'

Steph Houghton, England and Manchester City football captain

Do

Improving your fitness starts with tiny changes. As the habits expert James Clear puts it, the goal is to become '1 per cent better each day'. In the left-hand column below, write down your average weekly exercise routine – whether that's going to the gym every day, or just having the occasional stroll. Now, use the right-hand column to write down what small 1 per cent change you could make to that routine, whether it's running for five minutes longer, or walking another fifty metres. Small changes, you'll discover, can have outsized results.

Exercise routine	1 per cent better means . . .
Monday	
Tuesday	
Wednesday	
Thursday	
Friday	
Saturday	
Sunday	

Inspire

'During my workouts, I often talk about how I'm not in the mood for it . . . But I say, "Let's do it together – and by the end of it, we will feel better." That is the power of exercise.'

Joe Wicks, fitness coach, presenter, influencer and bestselling author

Think

Many of our high performers – from Zack George to Joe Wicks to John McAvoy – say that the trick to transforming your exercise habits in the long term is learning to enjoy working out. Easier said than done, you might think. But in our experience, most people – however athletic or unathletic – find that they enjoy certain types of exercise. You might love a gentle stroll or get high training for a five-kilometre race. In the space below, write down the last three times you remember enjoying exercise. What do your answers tell you about the right type of fitness for you?

_____

_____

_____

_____

_____

_____

Lesson round-up

Small changes compound. Over time, they lead to an exponential improvement in your abilities. But to keep that change ticking, you need to adopt the Japanese spirit of 'kaizen' – constant improvement. Keep upgrading your exercise routine every day, every month, every year. Do five more push-ups. Walk for three minutes longer. Cycle for one last mile. And, eventually, you'll have the same realisation as John McAvoy: that your mind, your body and your life are changing.

Reflections:

_____

_____

_____

_____

_____

_____

_____

_____

_____

_____

_____

_____

Culture

SPOTTING YOUR CULTURE

Last week's focus was **exercise**. We emphasised the power of small, achievable, healthy changes that can bolster your physical fitness. What did you learn?

_____

_____

_____

Think about your **goals** for the year. What have you done in the past week to help you achieve them?

_____

_____

_____

This week's focus is **spotting your culture**. Culture is the highest manifestation of a team's purpose – what drives some groups to thrive and others to fail. What does spotting your culture mean to you?

_____

_____

_____

Inspire

'You can have all the talent that God provides you – but without attitude, you won't achieve anything.'

Mauricio Pochettino, former manager of Paris Saint-Germain and Tottenham

Think

Former Tottenham manager Mauricio Pochettino said there were two things that could change the mood of a dressing room: energy and attitude. According to Pochettino, you need to give out the kind of energy that you want to define your life: the best teams have a relentlessly positive 'energia universal', as he put it. What kind of energy do you give out – and what effect do you think it has on your team's mood?

_____

_____

_____

_____

_____

_____

_____

_____

Do

Circle the words that you associate with your team's energy. Do you think there's a positive atmosphere or a negative one?

Optimistic	Enthusiastic	Defeatist	Fatalistic
Negative	Energetic	Constructive	Pessimistic
Gloomy	Confident	Welcoming	Loving
Happy	Drab	Cheerful	Encouraging

Inspire

'Even the best team in the world can crumble if they don't have that core structure.'

Angela Ruggiero, four-time Olympic ice hockey medallist

Think

Stanford professors James Baron and Michael Hannan investigated the effect of culture on a company's fortunes. In a vast study – which followed almost 200 companies over fifteen years – they concluded that culture was the best determinant of whether a business succeeds or fails. Think about places you have worked in the past. How would you characterise the culture of the best organisation?

Do

In their research, Baron and Hannan identified five different types of corporate culture: star, engineering, bureaucracy, autocracy and commitment, which consistently outperformed the rest. Can you think of examples of each type? Why do you think commitment cultures perform so well?

1. Star: getting the best employees is everything, and vast sums are spent recruiting the sharpest people.

   Example: _____

2. Engineering: the technicians and scientists are in control, and technical roles are the best rewarded.

   Example: _____

3. Bureaucracy: every decision is governed by rules, policies and convoluted systems.

   Example: _____

4. Autocracy: similar to bureaucracies, but all rules are in place to appease one, all-powerful figure (usually the CEO).

   Example: _____

5. Commitment: people work there because they have a strong connection to the organisation, believe in its purpose and like their colleagues.

   Example: _____

THE BIG WHY

Last week's focus was **spotting your culture**. We looked at positive team energy, and the five types of culture. What did you learn?

_____

_____

_____

Think about your **goals** for the year. What have you done in the past week to help you achieve them?

_____

_____

_____

This week's focus is **the big why**. The best teams build a commitment culture by having a clear sense of what they are _for_. What does finding the why mean to you?

_____

_____

_____

_____

Think

Way back in Lesson II, we discovered how long-term motivation comes from finding a sense of meaning, a cause that transcends just getting paid or being promoted. But this principle doesn't just apply to individuals – it applies to whole teams. Groups need to answer the 'why' question if they're going to pull together.

Reflect on your team. Why do they do what they do? What motivates them?

_____

_____

_____

_____

_____

_____

_____

_____

_____

Inspire

'You've got to pursue goals that are true to you.'

Harpreet Kaur, owner and co-founder of Oh So Yum,
and winner of The Apprentice

Do

To build a sense of commitment, a team needs to be able to answer that simple 'why' question – or, as we call it, 'The Big Why'. Over the next day or two, try asking three members of your team why they do what they do and record their answers below.

The person	The why

Inspire

'We always knew that we were playing for – and representing – every female in the country.'

Tracy Neville, manager of the England Roses netball team

Do

Of course, what we think is motivating us might not actually be what is motivating us. This exercise, developed by the founder of Toyota in the 1930s, will help you drill down to the root causes of our behaviour. It involves asking 'Why?' five times. By the fifth why, you should have a clear sense of what's really driving you.

Try it with an unexplained behaviour you've noticed in your team. Do the five whys help you get to the bottom of what's going on?

Why are you . . . ? _____

Why? _____

Why? _____

Why? _____

Why? _____

Think

Now turn from your team to other teams. Think of the most successful group you can – it can be a business competitor, a local sports team or a world-famous organisation. What is their Big Why? Is it clear to everyone who works there?

_____

_____

_____

EMOTIONAL INTELLIGENCE

Last week's focus was **find the why.** We explored how to find a team's purpose by answering 'The Big Why'. What did you learn?

_____

_____

_____

Think about your **goals** for the year. What have you done in the past week to help you achieve them?

_____

_____

_____

This week's focus is **emotional intelligence.** We are going to argue that the best cultures have a strong sense of emotional connection between members and explore how to build it. What does emotional intelligence mean to you?

_____

_____

_____

Inspire

'A simple look into the eyes of a teammate, letting them know you have their back, is a powerful feeling.'

Ian McGeechan, former rugby player and coach

Think

In a study by Carnegie Mellon University and MIT, a group of psychologists assessed how an emotional bond can affect a team's performance. It revealed that the best groups were those with high levels of emotional insight into one another. Researchers refer to this as 'emotional intelligence' or EQ – emotional quotient. It refers to the ability of a group to read one another's emotions, implicitly and unthinkingly. Do you think you have high EQ? Explain your answer.

_____

_____

_____

_____

_____

_____

_____

_____

Do

In the grid below list three of the people in your team. In the next column, score the level of emotional connection you feel you have with them on a scale of 1 (if you hardly know them) to 5 (if you know their kids' names, birthday and favourite TV shows). And then write how much you feel they know about you in the final column, too.

When members of a team know each other better and understand each other's emotions, they work together better because they know how to cooperate and feel more motivated. Does your team have strong emotional connections?

Name	My connection to them	Their connection to me

Think

Kevin Sinfield, the former captain of Leeds Rhinos rugby league team, was focused on building strong emotional bonds within the team he loved (he joined the club at the age of thirteen). Although on paper the club was never the best resourced or flashiest, it became the most successful league side in two decades.

Can you think of an organisation that overperforms? Do strong emotional connections within the team help to explain why?

_____

_____

_____

_____

_____

_____

_____

_____

_____

Inspire

'I always felt my job was to help people be better than they believe.'

Kevin Sinfield, former Leeds Rhinos player and one of the most awarded captains in rugby league history

Do

If you feel like you or your peers have low EQ, do not fear. Research has shown that you can build your emotional intelligence. It starts with paying attention. Below is a list of some questions to ask about members of your team: use a different person for each one. If you can't answer them now, find out the answers by talking to people. The goal is to develop a strong sense of how everyone around you is feeling – the essence of high EQ.

1. Does _____ seem comfortable?

    Answer: _____

2. Does _____ upset anyone?

    Answer: _____

3. When is _____'s birthday?

    Answer: _____

4. Does _____ have children?

    Answer: _____

5. Does _____ speak up before the group?

    Answer: _____

PSYCHOLOGICAL SAFETY

Last week's focus was **emotional intelligence.** We delved into why EQ is the secret ingredient for a high-performing culture. What did you learn?

_____

_____

_____

Think about your **goals** for the year. What have you done in the past week to help you achieve them?

_____

_____

_____

This week's focus is **psychological safety.** We are going to explore one of the most important characteristics of the best organisations' cultures: they make people feel safe, secure and able to take risks. What does psychological safety mean to you?

_____

_____

_____

Think

Amy Edmondson, an organisational psychologist at Harvard Business School, originally thought that a team that gelled well would make fewer mistakes. But, to her surprise, she found that the opposite seemed to be the case – the better teams were making more mistakes. It turned out that, in fact, the well-gelled teams were just more willing to *admit* to their mistakes: they had a strong sense of 'psychological safety'. Does your team feel like somewhere you can own up to your mistakes?

_____

_____

_____

_____

_____

_____

_____

Inspire

'Can you be vulnerable within your team? Can you show fear? And will you manage your own fear, to show up every day?'

Pippa Grange, former head of people and team development at the Football Association and advisor to the England football team

Do

List three mistakes or failures that you or others have made as part of a team and also list the fallout. Was there chastisement? Harsh words? Or was the mistake accepted, forgiven and learned from? In the best teams, people don't hold grudges. Everyone feels able to make mistakes, and so everyone is able to learn.

Mistake 1: _____

Fallout: _____

_____

Mistake 2: _____

Fallout: _____

_____

Mistake 3: _____

Fallout: _____

_____

Inspire

'Don't play with the fear of failure – play with the anticipation of success.'

Steve Clarke, manager of the Scottish national football team

Think

Tracey Neville wanted the England Roses netball team to feel comfortable failing in front of one another. 'If we wanted to win, we had to do things differently,' she told us. 'We had to get used to failing: failing fast and getting better.' Think about you and your team. Do you learn from your failures, or try to cover them up?

_____

_____

_____

_____

_____

_____

_____

_____

_____

_____

_____

_____

_____

_____

_____

_____

Do

When Damian was working with Tracey and the England Roses, they used a simple exercise to work out how psychologically safe the culture was. Every four weeks, they would ask the players to answer the below questions, borrowed from one of Amy Edmondson's seminal papers on psychological safety.

Try asking these questions about your own working life – or even ask them of your team. How psychologically safe is your environment? What could you do to build a sense of safety in each area?

1. *If I make a mistake on my team, do I feel it's held against me?* _____

_____

2. *Are my colleagues able to bring up problems and tough issues?* _____

_____

3. *Is it safe to take a risk?* _____

_____

4. *Is it difficult to ask other members of this team for help?* _____

_____

5. *When I am working with colleagues, do I feel my unique skills and talents are valued and used?*

_____

_____

LESSON IN REVIEW
CULTURE

Last week's focus was **psychological safety**. We looked at how the highest-performing cultures are those where people feel relaxed, and able to own up to their mistakes. What did you learn?

_____

_____

_____

Think about your **goals** for the year. What have you done in the past week to help you achieve them?

_____

_____

_____

This week we're going to summarise what we've learnt about **culture**. Has this lesson made you see it differently?

_____

_____

_____

Inspire

'Culture is created by people.'

Gareth Southgate, manager of the
England football team

Think

Gareth Southgate took over the England football team at a very low ebb. He steered them to two major semi-finals in successive tournaments. We'd put that down to the commitment culture he'd created, one in which everyone felt safe and valued.

Do you have a commitment culture in your team? If not, how will you create one? Draw on the suggestions from this lesson in your answer.

_____

_____

_____

_____

_____

_____

_____

_____

Do

Culture is created by the whole team, but that doesn't mean that leaders can abdicate responsibility. It is the job of leaders to set an example – so that their team can feel truly at home.

Think about a large team you're in. Write in the below circles what each person brings to the team – focusing on the positives. Next, reflect on what you've learnt in this chapter. How will you bring out these positive characteristics in each person?

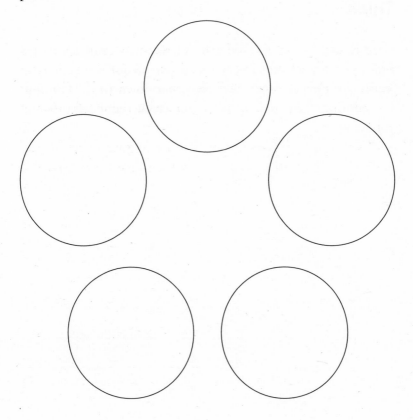

Inspire

'My job as a coach is to get them to be their best – and then try and improve that level.'

Steve Borthwick, head coach of Leicester Tigers rugby team

Think

Culture can be the hardest part of high performance to get right, because it's not just about what you do, or what your leader does – it's about what the whole team does. How will you educate the people around you about the importance of good culture?

_____

_____

_____

_____

_____

_____

_____

_____

_____

Lesson round-up

Culture is everywhere, but we often ignore it. This is a mistake – because if you can forge a high-engagement 'commitment culture', high performance takes care of itself.

Three ingredients make for a strong commitment culture:

1. Meaning: people need a sense of purpose, so try to answer that simple, all-important question – why are we doing this?
2. Connection: attempt to boost the emotional bonds within a group. Take stock frequently: are your teammates happy or sad, motivated or demoralised?
3. Safety: team members must feel able to make mistakes. Don't hold grudges and learn to embrace failure.

Remember Gareth Southgate's rule: 'Culture is created by people.' And that means it's everyone's responsibility – from assistant to manager, secretary to CEO.

LEARNING

'Every person who's got somewhere has some teacher in their past who has inspired them,' the bestselling author Lee Child once told us on the podcast. But what does it mean to be a teacher? The term doesn't refer only to someone who imparts knowledge at the front of a classroom – it can mean so much more: an individual who nurtures us and helps us grow, someone we respect and who, in return, respects us, someone who draws upon their own mistakes to prevent us repeating them.

These teachers, we have found in our interviews, can be found everywhere. In our schools, yes, but also in our jobs, our hobbies and our families. As would-be high performers, our obligation is to seize the opportunity to learn from these teachers and to apply their wisdom in our own lives. This, perhaps, is the most important trait of high performance: having the *will* to learn.

Because learning is not something that stops when you leave school or university. It is a key ingredient in unlocking our potential – the force that allows us to develop new skills, take on new ideas and become our best. And, fortunately enough, we can learn how to learn. According to academics at Stanford University, effective teaching and learning requires three ingredients: a growth mindset, a sense of belonging in our learning environment and an understanding of why what we're learning matters.

We've already encountered these ideas in this journal – whether in the week about finding your 'why', or in the material about Carol Dweck's theory of mindset. Here, we'll examine how to apply them in the context of education so that the road to high performance becomes one of constant learning. When we understand how to learn, we can live up to the ideals brought out by our most admired teachers.

Reflections:

_____

_____

_____

_____

_____

_____

_____

_____

_____

_____

_____

_____

_____

_____

_____

_____

_____

_____

Think

Not everyone enjoys formal education, but most people can think of a learning environment – whether a school, a sports team or a company – where they picked up some useful knowledge. When did you last feel like you were learning a lot? What was it about that environment that made you feel able to learn?

_____

_____

_____

_____

_____

_____

_____

_____

_____

_____

Inspire

'One golden rule: be curious, be the learner.'

Rangan Chatterjee, doctor, author and podcast host

Do

Part of finding a learning environment where you belong is about knowing the type of team you thrive in. In our experience, most learning methods fall into one of the following categories:

- Top-down: where a teacher tells students what to do.
- Participatory: where a teacher invites every member of the group to chime in with their ideas.
- Democratic: where no one leads the group and everyone participates equally.

Some learning environments have all three characteristics at different times. In the Venn diagram below, fill in your own educational experiences – whether at school, at work or anywhere else. In which environment did you thrive? How can you use that knowledge to drive your learning further?

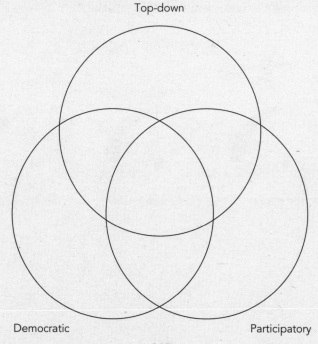

Top-down

Democratic

Participatory

Inspire

'I am always learning. I don't have all the answers now, but I will find an answer.'

Vex King, motivational speaker, author and influencer

Do

As the Stanford learning model shows, picking up new skills is down to a growth mindset, a sense of belonging and the power of meaning. But these three criteria will matter in different proportions to different people. On the below gauges, mark how important each element feels to your learning journey. What is really driving you to better yourself?

Growth mindset   Belonging   Meaning

Lesson round-up

Learning is a lifelong process – but only if you notice it. As Lee Child told us, the trick is to 'realise that you've learnt something and that your life was shifted – and then keep yourself open to that possibility.' This can happen at any age or stage, and, as Child notes, 'It might happen again.' As you reach the end of your high-performance journey, keep noticing what you're learning. The enemy of high performance is inattentiveness. Only by knowing what we've learnt so far will we be able to learn again.

Reflections:

_____

_____

_____

_____

_____

_____

_____

_____

_____

_____

_____

_____

_____

The Call to Courage

THE CALL TO COURAGE

Last week's focus was **learning**. We explored that learning isn't something limited to our youth – it's a lifelong process. What did you learn?

_____

_____

_____

Think about your **goals** for the year. What have you done in the past week to help you achieve them?

_____

_____

_____

This week's focus is **the call to courage.** Courage is the final ingredient of high performance – a characteristic that lurked, quiet and unassuming, in the background of every single one of our interviews. What does the call to courage mean to you?

_____

_____

_____

Inspire

'High performance is about presence. I feel I am a high performer if I can be present in everything that I'm doing.'

Rangan Chatterjee, doctor, author and podcast host

Think

Becoming a high performer requires change. And change is scary. You need courage to get there. But what actually is courage? It's not so much never feeling fear, as feeling fear and still pushing through. Use this space to reflect on moments of courage from your life. When have you felt bravest?

_____

_____

_____

_____

_____

_____

_____

_____

_____

_____

Do

So, how can we build true courage – the kind that involves embracing rather than supressing our fear? Based on asking dozens of high performers about overcoming fear, we have come up with a simple toolkit:

1. Ask for help: high performance can be lonely, but solutions often come from people we trust.
2. Believe in yourself: remember how far you've come and how much you've achieved.
3. Look fear in the eye: perhaps we can't eradicate our fear of failing, but we can embrace it.

Use the below table to reflect on how you will build courage in each of these areas. True courage is within your reach.

Ask for help	Believe in yourself	Look fear in the eye

Inspire

'It's a gift to find things in life that we can be committed to. It gives us a compass.'

Matthew McConaughey, Oscar-winning actor

Think

The key to Gareth Southgate's success, he told us, was simple: authenticity. 'I think our league is rich with some of the best coaches in the world. They've all got different ways but they've got to be themselves – it's got to be the way that's authentic to them,' he said. 'People smell it a mile off if you're not yourself.' In our opinion, that is the highest form of courage: being true to yourself. Use the space below to reflect on what it means to you to be authentic.

_____

_____

_____

_____

_____

_____

_____

_____

_____

Do

Authenticity differs from person to person, and from team to team. In the space below, write the names of three high performers you admire. Next, reflect on what makes each one authentic in their approach. How do they stay true to themselves? Does each person adopt a different approach?

High performer 1:

_____

Authentic through ...

_____

_____

_____

_____

_____

_____

_____

_____

_____

_____

High performer 2:

_____

Authentic through ...

_____

_____

_____

_____

_____

_____

_____

_____

_____

_____

High performer 3:

_____

Authentic through ...

_____

_____

_____

_____

_____

_____

_____

_____

_____

_____

THE YEAR IN REVIEW

Last week's focus was **the call to courage**. We tried to show that true courage isn't about suppressing fear – it's about embracing it. What did you learn?

_____

_____

_____

Think about your **goals** for the year. What have you done in the past week to help you achieve them?

_____

_____

_____

It's our final week, and that means it's time for **the year in review**. Think back to how you felt at the beginning of your high-performance year. How do you feel the year has been?

_____

_____

_____

Think

Cast your mind back to when you started the book. How do you feel you have changed over the past year? Do you feel your life has moved in the right direction?

_____

_____

_____

_____

_____

_____

_____

_____

_____

_____

_____

Inspire

'Life is a verb. Go and live it.'

Matthew McConaughey, Oscar-winning actor

Do

Look back at the goals you set for yourself in week 2. In the below table, give yourself a score out of 10 for how well you achieved each goal and record your reflections on what you've learnt. How far have you come in your journey to high performance?

	Goal	Score	Reflections
1.			
2.			
3.			

Inspire

'High performance encompasses all aspects of competition, and of life.'

Christian Horner, team principal of Red Bull F1 and winner of nine world titles

Do

We can think of high performance as a flywheel. It takes a lot of energy to get the wheel turning – but the more it turns, the easier it is to keep it going. Your actions over the last year are no different. At times, it will have felt like you're making slow progress. But when it comes to high performance, every small action counts. On the left-hand side of the diagram below, write down how your actions this year will feed into your long-term journey to high performance. On the right-hand side, reflect on what you'll do next year to keep the flywheel turning.

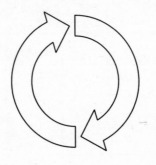

Think

We've reached the end of our high-performance year. I hope the exercises in this book have helped you get a little closer to the life you want to lead. More than that, we hope you've discovered something about your mindset, your behaviour and your goals. Reflect on what you've learnt about yourself in the space below.

Remember, high performance is never about lying to yourself. It's about becoming yourself. We hope that by joining us over the past year, you've learnt a little more about who you really are.

The year ahead

Congratulations on completing the high-performance journal. But high performance never stops: no matter how far you've come, there's always further to go. Use this space to reflect on how you'll apply the lessons you've learnt over the year ahead.

_____

_____

_____

_____

_____

_____

_____

_____

_____

_____

_____

_____

_____

_____

_____

_____

_____

Notes

NOTES

CONTINUE YOUR
HIGH PERFORMANCE JOURNEY

Buy another
High Performance journal
for the year ahead

Read the
High Performance
book

Listen to the *High
Performance* podcast

Watch the *High Performance*
YouTube series

Learn about the *High
Performance* project

Join the *High Performance*
members club